DIVORCE
The First Six Months
with Peter Maestrey

I want to welcome you.

Today is a beginning for what you create.

Copyright © 2023

All rights reserved. No part of this book may be
reproduced, scanned, or distributed in any printed or
electronic form without permission.

If you find yourself without the time or focus to read. This book was written as a result of my podcast. Sometimes listening to others also provides us a road to travel on while we are experiencing divorce. If you find this to be true. I invite you to listen when you have time. This podcast is the story of many who have endured a divorce and how they coped and built from it.

www.divorcethefirstsix.com

Dear Reader.

What I came up with was NOT to make a table of contents. You are here because you want to know about divorce. My guess is that you want to understand what is required of you in divorce, and the divorce process.

Divorce takes time and it takes patience. It takes knowing your strength, and weakness, but also understanding them. The table of contents was removed so that you don't rush this book.

My request is for you to give yourself the time it takes to get where you are going.

I understand there will likely be a certain aspect of divorce that's affecting you significantly right now—whether it's the heartbreak, the loneliness, dealing with high conflict with your ex, or trying to get to grips with co-parenting, for example. I am weary that if I were to give you a contents table, you may well be tempted to jump right in at a certain page to try to find the best advice you can that's going to help you. And I get it, your heart may be racing, there might be tears in your eyes and you're scrambling through the shattered dream trying to pick up the pieces and keep sane. However, I'd like to invite you to just breathe your way through this book in its entirety. Relax into it and take this not as just a quick bit of advice, but rather as some quality time for you—time which you can view as an investment in your overall well-being.

Depending on how quickly you read, you can likely read this whole book in less than a few hours. So, here, I ask you to trust me with this. I believe that what you're really seeking is a comprehensive review of the world that divorce presents us with, not just a few paragraphs that may help you here and there.

Let me share with you all that I learned, the good, the bad, and the ugly..

On that note, I'll pause here while you make yourself comfortable, and when you are ready we'll begin…

I'm grateful you continued.

Welcome to divorce. If this book is where you are choosing to start, continue, or complete the divorce process, you are in the right place. Thank you for reading "Divorce: The First Six Months."

The purpose of this book is to shine a light on what you can expect to experience, specifically within the first six months of a divorce. Sharing stories and insights from the perspective of strengthening the mind, body, and soul as it moves along the divorce process. The goal is that you, the reader, by the end of the book has a better understanding of what happens to you during this time.

Through this book, I will give you tools you can use as you journey through the first six months of your divorce, with the aim of sharpening your focus so you may manage your day to day life with a sense of structure and clarity.

I would also like to take a moment to clarify that I am not a therapist, I am not a guru, nor am I a certified mental anything professional. I am a man who went through it, documented every step, and then created a successful podcast and business from the experience. I recognized something about the system already in place which was missing. So, I decided to pass on my learnings and offer this book as a support for anyone who finds themselves journeying a similar path and stepping out into unknown and seemingly unstable territory.

The healing process doesn't have a defined shape or size, but it can be measured with time and acceptance. The more time you place into understanding yourself inside the divorce and educating yourself on what you want from it, the smoother it is to reach acceptance. Acceptance, I believe, is the ultimate understanding you can achieve to transition yourself into the future you want. The best you.

I believe you are here because you are looking for a way to educate yourself about divorce; to guide yourself towards a future that is not defined at this exact moment, and to learn how to navigate all the decisions that will soon be before you. I think all these assumptions and more are addressed inside the pages of this book. I believe you will find some, if not all the answers on what to expect inside the first six months of a divorce.

This book was written to ignite you into exploring who you are today as you begin to ask yourself who do you want to be tomorrow. Searching where you lost yourself inside the relationship, or life in general, we will then build on how you can create who you want to be in the future.

My hope is that through exploring the memory of who you were, you're going to start nurturing yourself into becoming a bigger, stronger, and wiser version of who you are today. All the while, learning the process and the needed steps to take.

If you are ready, let's begin shaping the you that you want to be…

THE BIG PICTURE

Checking in with yourself

Divorce is going to be about you, and more importantly, who you choose to be inside of it. How you think, how you make choices, how you react to things, and everything in between that will drive the divorce process. How you navigate through the divorce will determine who you become after it is complete. If you make decisions out of resentment, you will be resentful. If you make choices in anger, you will be angry. But if you create with acceptance, then you will be accepting. How you make decisions, and more importantly, who you are inside of those decisions is what you have a great deal of power over.

It's important to remember that you got you here, and it's you who is going to be there when the divorce is over. The book will point out the bumps on the road we call "divorce", but it will be up to you to slow down, or speed up as you approach those bumps.

I want you to imagine for a moment that your spouse has nothing to do with who you get to be inside the divorce. Consider you are the only person who has the power to decide this. Who do you want to be? Who would you like to be?

Take a moment to check in with yourself and see what's really happening. What are you feeling? Who are you?

I want to invite you to practice being mindful of what is around you, to be an observer in your life. Begin to look at life as you would a play, or an event. It is when you start to look at life from a different perspective that you will begin to have different results.

For example, are you aware of how you come across to other people, how they view you? Are you aware of what you look like when you talk to them about your situation or how you listen? Do you think you are a good listener, do you think you listen?

Do you notice what triggers you to behave differently around your spouse, in comparison to others, or with friends? Do you look people in the eye when speaking to them? Do they look you in the eye? Are you aware of how you react when you're feeling scared, uncertain, or alone? How do you react when you are confident, poised, or empowered?

Begin to see yourself through the eyes of others, see your strengths along with your weaknesses; notice how you manage yourself; write it down, remember it, or instigate conversations about this with others.

In this book, we are going to check the many things that could have an influence on who you are, who you were, and more importantly, who you want to be.

We are going to explore what you are feeling, thinking, and doing. Looking at the triggers, identifying them, and then taking actions from a perspective of being outside of ourselves.

Checking in with yourself will allow you to see what you are saying to yourself, and to others, and what it is that you actually want to say. This is your time to study and evaluate what is around you; an opportunity to merge what you are thinking with what you are saying, and being assured that what you are both thinking and saying represent your intention.

This will create a foundation where you can be clear on the communication that you want to share. If this sounds appealing, keep reading.

Ask yourself 'What happened?'

"What happened?" is a question you are going to ask yourself for quite some time and it is perfectly normal for it to exist in your thoughts, in your conversation, and most importantly within you—especially within you.

In my opinion, you shouldn't avoid it, you should embrace it. I'll explain why as we continue, but for now, imagine this adventure called 'Divorce' to be a movie you're watching. And as with every movie, it starts with learning about the main character—which happens to be you. When we meet the protagonist, we learn about what makes them who they are, and we witness them facing some kind of dilemma—which at this moment is you looking out at the world and asking the question: "What happened?"

Allow me to share my "What happened?" as it occurred for me when I was standing in your place at the beginning of my Divorce movie. There is no right or wrong way of asking and managing this question, but maybe you can see what I am saying by reading my story.

In the moment, when my now Ex-wife said the magical words to me "I don't know if I love you anymore", my entire world shattered The only consistent recurring question from that moment in my life was asking myself, "What happened?" My heart and my thoughts became mush. It was the stillest my life had ever been and I was lost.

I asked myself 'Why?' as I drove to work, as I made dinner, or as I was listening to someone talk while my mind wandered.

I explored scenarios of what happened, I questioned my commitments, and I overanalyzed my thoughts of every memory I had from the moment I met her till the present day.

Looking back now, even if she had explained what had happened to us, I would still have asked myself the same question. "What happened?"

is what we ask ourselves to try and understand. It's the question you can ask over and over again and never get the answer you want to hear. Yet, it comforts you in an unexplainable way. It's a vicious loop of the same thoughts taking up space and time—time which you do not have to waste.

What I am about to write next might be difficult for you to accept, and you might need to read this sentence once or twice to really get what it means to you personally. I say this because it is not a logical sentence. I also say this because it robbed me of my time, and I do not wish the same to happen to you.

It doesn't make a difference to know what happened.

This is not to say knowing something might give you freedom or something else around the separation. It is saying that it doesn't make a difference towards what is really important—which is for you to have access to starting over with strength and confidence.

This book is created with the intention of speaking to the person within you who knows this divorce is happening and does not know what to expect, nor how to plan for it. The you which is unaware of the emotional roller coaster about to descend, taking you through loops and turns that will make your belly produce more emotions than you can plan for; the you in the movie, who learned devastating news and is at the point of loss, now facing a choice.

So, when you think of the question, "What just happened?"—which you will, and it could happen often—allow yourself to search, question, and observe what just happened. Entertain the question for as long as it takes up space inside your mind, but know that each time it occupies your mind, it is just a question, and that, in time, this question will be substituted with another one. What is important is to allow it to move through you while observing what it is you want from knowing the answer to this question.

How to Stay Positive

Staying positive is a generated action, much like "fake it till you make it." You have to cause it, to will it, and most importantly to be the source of it. It is born in the moments you do not wish to be kind or appreciative, but know deep inside that there will be a better outcome if you were to create either of those. It is the smile that you build on top of the pain embodying you. It is the scream you silence or substitute with a nod of "yes or no". I want to invite you to not wait for any of these to arrive: build it.

Start with a smile, then a laugh. Remember the things which make these emotions happen for you and then do them. Regardless of what the reality might be of the moment, change the reality towards your terms by being what you wish to be.

For example, say you are mistreated by your spouse and it was mean, rude, and not something you agree with. How do you react? How do you interpret what happened? What do you do with the circumstances inside that moment?

You have two choices in these moments, you can create or react. If you react to the moment, much of the same which led you here will happen. It is probable that you will continue to receive the same outcome. Each trying to be heard while the other keeps speaking. More of the same. Whereas, if you create inside this circumstance you have the ability to try something new, something different. If you create what you wish the moment to be, and do the work to will it, then you have something different.

Your power is in knowing who you are, what you want, and what you are willing to tolerate (and where to draw the lines in the sand) that gives you access to confidence. Confidence is the fuel you will use to create being positive. It is the fuel you will need to create.

It is knowing that allows us to be calm and poised inside these moments of uncertainty. It is asking ourselves the difficult questions and having a future we can describe in detail that fuel this positive nature. It is understanding what we are willing to surrender and what we are not that allow us to communicate with a sense of purpose. This is all part of creations DNA.

When we look at the most successful humans in history for reference. It was their vision that drove their futures through the muddy obstacles of the day to day. Your vision, what you want to create as the finalization of the divorce is your blue print, your map, your idea.

From placing a man on the moon to today's social media. It all began with an idea, but it was the perseverance that delivered on the promise of the idea. It was speaking it into existence that created the first steps. Your idea of life after divorce is the seed you are planting because you know together is no longer an option. Close your eyes and imagine the life you want in lieu of the life you have.

What makes carrying the weight of divorce somewhat bearable is knowing it takes time to begin living a new life—one that we will love more than the present. But, it also takes thought and contemplation; it takes planning; it takes time to heal and also to participate. It takes time to recreate what you want and most importantly, what you're worth to create staying positive.

It takes time and a conscious effort to stay positive. Be mindful that you can create being positive, it is your choice.

What to expect from Grieving

You are going to want to grieve. You need to grieve. You are about to move on and start a life that doesn't have that other person next to you romantically, physically, or emotionally. You are completing the life you had with this person, so grieving should be expected and acknowledged.

Like every beginning, there is an end. To complete the process means that all the steps have been taken; you have done everything there was to do.

Like a test with ten questions, if you answered all ten, the test is complete. Like washing clothes, once the dryer stops, the process is complete. Grieving is a part of completing your situation. It is saying goodbye with your mind, your body, and your soul.

These are some of the questions you should consider asking yourself to open up the conversation for grieving. As you ask these questions or questions of your own, always consider the exercise to be an opportunity to explore what you are feeling. To allow them to exist without judgement, so you can observe.

How do you manage the feeling of loss? How do you trust that you will eventually be okay and that life will eventually move on? How do you allow time to take its course? How much time will it take and how do you know when it's complete? What is the correct way of grieving? Is there a correct way? Am I hurt?

All of us are different. We are all individuals when it comes to this process and could approach it differently. My belief is that however you choose to grieve is yours. My only concern around this emotional stage would be that you do not blame yourself, or others. That you observe yourself and then apply or withdrawal the elements that make you a better version of yourself.

During this time, my advice would be to stay present, to be responsible and accountable for your part inside this process. Allow yourself to be with the loss, to be with the memories, and then ask yourself what you need in order to stop grieving.

When I attempted to not allow myself to grieve, or to make something wrong in the process of my divorce, I was removed from my healing. It was when I remembered who she was, who I was in the marriage, when I discovered that divorce was neither mine or her fault. It was just part of the process. I did not have the need to grieve anymore once I remembered who she was, and who I had the opportunity to be. Till this day remembering brings me comfort. It allowed me to accept divorce as part of our process in lieu of blaming or making it wrong.

During my grief period, my perspective shifted from blaming myself and her for what was happening, to missing what was now leaving me— which was what I really wanted to say. I was going to miss my wife and her daughter. I was saying goodbye to a family I treasured.

You could dwell on the negative, or you can dwell on the positive. You can grieve and move on, or you can grieve and stay still.

You have the choice to entertain the things which do not work, or you can entertain the ideas that do work. The fact of the matter is that divorce is the end of something and healing is what comes next, and that takes time. Don't pollute your time with negative thoughts. Give yourself permission to feel whatever emotion may come up from the memories you made and like a glass of water when you drink it, let it flow through you until it's released.

Embrace the emotions which rise up from who knows where and stay positive, and if you have nothing nice to say, stay quiet—there's no sense in stirring things up as you go through your process.

Grieving is your process to own it. From witnessing the exact ways grief shows up, to how you choose to manage it, so be mindful of how you want it to exist. It is when we refuse to accept the loss when grieving becomes unbearable, uncomfortable, and just plain 'un—'.

However you choose to grieve your loss, I hope you choose to do it with love, with respect, and with kindness. I hope that your choice leads you towards acceptance.

What to expect from Counseling

The beauty of having a professional listening to you speak is the amount of access you will have to what is **NOT** being said or recognized by you and your spouse. Having someone dedicated to listening to what you say is like having Elon Musk coach you in how to build an electric car.

Making the best possible decision with the least amount of risk cannot be made by guessing, or waiting for someone else to do something. It begins with educating yourself and asking questions that shape your future. It begins with identifying what you are not aware of and having people challenge you. Counseling could provide these challenges.

What do you keep inside a safe? Valuables? What you say and how you say it, is like a safe. A paid professional listening to you is the combination that gets you into that safe.

If you have the opportunity to use counseling, consider the costs and payoffs involved before taking the plunge. Don't go into it without a plan. Take the time to make a list of what you wish to achieve, and if you are not a list maker, then be extremely conscious of why you are going, what you wish to gain, and how much you are willing to spend in the following areas: financially, emotionally, and time.

For me, counseling was like shaking a snow globe. As the snowflakes began to fall down onto the small town of my life, you could see why and where the pieces landed as a result of my shaking it up. Each session was a different shake, building upon the previous one. I had good times, as well as bad, but they all gave me insight into something, and took me, step by step, closer to where I needed to be—which was "it's okay".

It's okay that I'm getting a divorce. It's okay that I am confused about why it happened. It's okay that I am scared of being alone. It's okay that I don't want to go find someone else. It's okay that I have an abundance of things to do to complete the divorce process. It's okay that I don't want to do anything. It's okay that I'm lost. It's okay that I'm looking for answers. It's okay that I don't know what I am doing. It's okay that I… You get the meaning of this: It was okay.

If you are attending, or planning to attend counseling under the belief you will be proven right or similar, save your money. I promise you, whatever reason you may have as to why you are not to blame, or why you harbor toxic hope, will never make a difference unless you begin to take responsibility for yourself and your actions.

To achieve an understanding of what is not understood, we must be ready to listen and also be responsible for what we can see. If you want to see results that have value, don't go to counseling with any other purpose than to explore who you are, what you are, and what you wish to be. This is about healing, not about being righteous. Counseling is about learning your patterns, your way of being, and what is stopping you from being the best version of yourself.

Asking yourself, what do I want?

Asking the question "What do I want?" has about as much color as a blank canvas when you are navigating a divorce. So, don't be hard on yourself if you don't know your answer immediately; clarity comes with time. I had all the colors of the world to paint with and yet I could not bring myself to decide on what it was I wanted to paint with my divorce.

I think this section's value will be solely dependent on how you interpret it, how you implement it, and what you choose to create from it. Many of us don't really understand how or why this question is important to our new beginning, so I am sharing my story in hopes that it can guide you. I'll show you how I came upon asking myself this question and what I created after asking. I'll begin at my day one.

On July 27th of 2019, I thought I had everything I wanted, till I heard her say she didn't know if she loved me. Immediately, I was lost and without a compass and the days began stacking. Even if I had known what I wanted, I would not have known how to get to what was next.

I was in and out of my emotions when it came to what needed to be done, thought of, or planned for. I was not skilled in what needed to be done within the divorce process. It made me scared to be clueless.

So, I did the only thing I knew I could do. I called a good friend who had experienced a very dramatic divorce and I began crying. In my eyes, he had a very successful, non dramatic divorce—afterall, he still talks to his ex, in spite of her doing some less than favorable things to him.

With him, I was able to begin looking into this question of what do I want and objectively answer it amidst the turmoil that was inside me. His sage advice led me to look at the big picture with a smaller, more bite sized approach. looking at the overall situation from what I knew, what was knowledge instead of what was in my head. It was soothing to look at it from a different perspective.

I began by writing down the obvious things first. The things that we owned. From the plates and silverware to the furniture and cars. Then, I moved onto the things that we shared, like our home, gym memberships, and a business.

Once that was complete, I circled back to the most important question: What did I want from this experience, from this divorce?

Having a list of all the possesions before me paved a path towards asking what I wanted spiritually. At this point, I really wanted to be okay with my soon to be ex not choosing me. I wanted to be okay with it, not conceptually, but for real. I didn't want to deny her the choice of not wanting to be with me, nor did I want to become difficult, or resent her for not choosing me. I guess I did not want to be like so many others I had seen in their divorce process: poisoning themselves and others with their complaints of what life had dealt them.

I wanted to be inspired and accepting of whatever may come of this new reality. I wanted to have love in my heart and to also untangle the knots of anger and confusion which embodied me. I wanted to be loving and kind.

When you know what you want, you create less confusion; you start to react less to what is happening, and the path forward begins to reveal itself with more clarity. You also don't get triggered by the other person as much, and I like to believe it is because you are no longer lost. You have access to a sense of direction which is calming. It wasn't easy to get there. I had to do the work, and you will, too… But I can say with assurance. Once I knew what I wanted, the choice to be loving and kind was 100% within my reach.

Are you okay with what you want?

Once you know what you want and begin to start living your life in alignment with your new goals, you should expect others will notice and act accordingly towards you. They will know what you expect of them and of yourself. Asking yourself if you are okay with what you want, could be an important question to consider once you define what it is you really want. Often times we do not consider if we are okay with our decisions or analyze or observe how we as an individuals feel about it.

Sometimes we create a plan and then change our minds, altering the steps to achieve it, and causing a ripple effect of things we don't want, or didn't invite. Knowing what we want from our divorce and seeing the bigger picture allows you to have a solid foundation in your thought and action process: a state of mind in which you can make decisions from a place of power in lieu of reactions.

For instance, when I found myself thinking, "I just want her to be happy." I did everything within my ability to make that happen. I said yes to every request, and I did so with a smile. Almost immediately my comfort level started to decline, which, within a rational mind we can imagine is bound to happen. My boundaries were getting pushed way past my preferred limits. I was giving up things like sleeping in the bedroom, my free time, and many other things that were important to me in my healing process. And I was doing it clearly for her comfort, not mine.

It wasn't until I realized her being happy was something I wanted that I could grasp onto the truth of what I needed . I wasn't confused about wanting to be with her, nor was I confused about choosing to make it work. I wanted her to be my wife and to stay married. But that was not going to happen, so I had to drop my longing for an impossible future and realize what I now wanted, which was for me to be okay, to be loving and kind. Her being happy was something for her to create.

It's important to mention that what I wanted also changed daily, sometimes hourly. It wasn't until I really gave it thought and captured it on paper that I began to see and feel the details of me wanting to be loving and kind inside the process and what that would actually look like.

By my standards, when I began sharing my thoughts with my trusted supporters, I began to comprehend I was giving up way more than I wanted to. I was assisting her in more ways than I was wanting to or wishing to be committed to. My intuition was clearly informing me that her integrity was not in line with mine.

I did not want to sleep on the couch. I did not want to take care of her daughter while she slept away from home. I was not committed to sharing a credit card, nor not knowing her whereabouts while traveling abroad. This began to be unacceptable as I identified what I was okay with, and more importantly, what I was not okay with.

If I had been clear on my boundaries and what was acceptable to me from the outset, I wouldn't have given more than I was comfortable with, nor ended up in a false peace, where I gave in but then resented the actions I was taking just to try to make my ex happy.

My access to my behavior and frame of mind was identifying what my truth was. Aligning my actions around what I believed, wanted, and thought was a fair compromise for all. Choosing this course of self-worth meant that I would be the deciding factor for my fate, so taking the bedroom back was the first step.

I spoke with her in a calm and intentional manner and stated clearly that I will be sleeping in the bedroom and understood if she needed to sleep elsewhere. After that moment, I never slept on the couch again.

I share my story simply to highlight the contemplation and actions that were necessary in order for me to make a shift in my life—a shift that pulled me up from my doormat status and into a mindset which I knew had the right to be happy and comfortable just as much as my ex did.

Being okay with what you want takes a conscious mind to determine, understand, and also to choose being okay with. It is not something that you should expect to wake up with one morning, feeling magically revived and confident. It takes being mindful and checking in with yourself regularly to recognize how you're feeling. It takes looking into the future and painting a picture of what you want, not what you have. First you must think it and dream it, before you can build it. As a result, I learned that I was more than okay with what I wanted.

Asking yourself 'What did I do?'

"What did I do?" another question that likely lurks in the back of your mind as you go about your day. A cousin to "What happened?", but a bit more self deprecating. A thought pattern which wonders if there is a way to fix the marriage. You begin to search for solutions and in the process become someone you might not be meant to be to save what might not need saving.

Inside this question if you might find yourself searching for where you could have done more, been more, or could still do more to turn things around, be wary.

For example, if you find yourself doing and saying things that only benefit or comfort the other person. Wherein, the lack of benefits is left on you. Such as, the burden of doing something you do not wish to do for the reward of being liked or appreciated, be wary.

When you look at the past memories hoping to find a clue as to where it began to go wrong in the relationship. You might begin to lose the focus as to why you are in this very moment. Chasing the ghost of who you once were. These are all paths that could lead to a future you do not want. Focus on the now and who you now are in lieu of what you did or who you were.

If you find yourself inside this loop, take a moment to check in with yourself and ask what you did. Look at what emotion is dominating you and be honest with yourself. Ask yourself what you did and then log it, read it, and at a later time study it. Take responsibility for all of it. Were you mean to your ex?, Were you a pushover? Did your absence cause a drift, or were you giving too much and suffocating your ex? Ask yourself the questions and answer them with sincerity. Then decide whether they are true and what you wish to do about them.

Be careful of fixing your marriage. If you are reading this book you need to consider that something in the marriage is leading you towards divorce and the marriage is not working.

Viewing it from what is not working might give you a greater sense of what to work on. When you ask yourself "what did I do" you might want to open this question up to your significant other and just listen to what they believe happened. Asking yourself will only provide you with your opinions, which then turn towards fixing. Many of us fall victim to this pattern because we avoid the silence that it takes to listen to someone we love tell us their point of view.

So my request is when you see yourself asking this question, don't. Open up the conversation with your spouse and listen to what they say as if your life depends on it. Don't defend or make wrong, don't tell them what you think or what your thoughts are, just listen. Listen to what and how they are saying what they say. What did I do is an empty sentence filled with blame and no freedom.

Asking yourself what can I do?

At the beginning of my divorce, I remember speaking to my friend and him saying I needed to get my head and heart to focus on a goal, an action, or a new activity—something that would assist me in getting my mind distracted in the upcoming year as I navigated the inevitable storm ahead.

He shared how jiu-jitsu had helped him; how journaling and envisioning the future he wanted (rather than the reality he had) was effective for him while he went through his divorce. He explained that creating his vision was important for him, because it was the part of life that made him feel safe, regardless of what was happening around him. He expressed how the ambition to manifest a new goal moved him.

I remember, when I was there for him, when he was going through his divorce, how much I admired his outlook and behavior, and how heart-warming it was to witness the many colorful spaces he often walked through while having to continuously participate in his bleak surroundings.

Regardless of whether he wanted those surroundings or not, he viewed them as an opportunity. He was raising two beautiful girls; full time. The mom was starting in a new relationship and surrendered raising the little ones while she traveled and nurtured her new life without him.

He had lots to say and be righteous about but, instead, he would call his trusted circle to vent, cry, and then create something new that would work for him, his kids, and his divorce—In turn, creating a better, more communicative future for all of them.

It's not an easy task to take on when you feel broken and alone, yet it is quite feasible when you look to the future you want for answers, rather than placing blame towards the past.

So I would like to invite you to consider that divorce is either a CREATION or a REACTION once again. What I mean by this is simple, you can create the divorce you would like to have, or you can react to the things that will arise as a result of the divorce.

If you consider everything that happens starting with either of these, you will find solace in your alignment. You will have a way of receiving new information or actions from a place of strength. For example, when I served my then wife with the divorce papers I was creating my future. A future she had agreed to weeks earlier. A future she had created which did not have me in it. I took the role of creating our divorce and in doing so began the steps that come with the territory.

Had I taken the reaction approach, I would've had to wait to be served or lingered about till she created something. In this particular example, had I not chosen to create I would've delayed my divorce. As a result of choosing to create, I was divorced six months after that action was taken.

You can cater to the other person, or you can begin to create the future you want. You can blame yourself and feel bad, or you can blame the other person. You can forgive yourself, or you can forgive the other person. You can join a gym, or cancel a gym membership. You can learn something new, or choose to do something you have put off for a long time. You can make a bucket list, or start scheduling your bucket list. You can complain about your situation, or you can get help. You can pretend like nothing is happening, or you can accept that it is happening. You have a lot of options regarding what you can do. Any direction you choose starts with choice.

It starts with choosing to do something and then taking the next steps, and the next, to begin and then maintain moving forward. Recognize the new life that's calling out to you and begin creating the steps to move towards it. Every moment that you are not creating for yourself is a moment you surrender to reacting.

So when you find yourself asking what can I do. Look at the piece of paper where you decided to create your life and begin doing that. The other option I guarantee you will not likely go the way you planned. Besides, it's not what you wish to create, why travel down that road.

Understanding Blame

Blame is a poison you drink, and get drunk on while the stories you tell yourself keep you thirsty. One of the greatest set backs most divorces have is the plentiful stories of how blame keeps them from moving on. Like a roadblock on your way to work in rush hour traffic.

When you're experiencing a breakdown, Blame can easily raise its head—often without us even realizing it. Creeping into the cracks of a bleeding heart like a virus taking hold, Blame negatively impacts our thoughts as it compels us to identify who was wrong, who was at fault, or who should have done something differently… and all these allegations lingering in the clouds of an already fogged mind do little to nothing to raise your mindfulness.

It's not always easy to recognize when we've entered into BlameMode, especially when feeling sad or defeated. Often, we have to be triggered by an external party to see what we're actually doing to ourselves and wise up to how we're behaving. Once we realize that we are wallowing, orBlaming, we can then adjust our focus, and change the game to create something healthier—something that is empowering us instead of disempowering.

Are you aware of what you can do to see blame? How you can you distinguish it before it is too late?

Are you able to list out who you blame and what you blame them for?

Can you recognize the difference between being lost in a witch hunt searching frantically for the guilty party, while being present with yourself in reality?

We are creatures of habit and when we're hurt, it's a natural knee-jerk reaction to see information to justify or explain who is responsible for this mess that we now find ourselves in..

Blame is a part of the process, and no matter whether you're blaming yourself or the other person, it doesn't tend to produce a positive result—rather it gives way to a false sense of knowledge as it makes you consider that you are right. And the other person is wrong.

Does it make you feel better to sit mentally assessing the situation as judge and jury calculating who did what "wrong", or does it prolong your healing process? Can you answer this question with certainty?

Shortly after my divorce was understood and my spouse and I began taking actions and making choices that moved us in that direction, I began fact checking my thoughts, her words, and the observations coming from friends and family. I began actively asking myself where the blame was to rest. Exploring all avenues that led me to and from blame. Looking at the relationship from the perspective of where I could make repairs or take responsibility.

I was no longer plagued with feelings of being responsible for her happiness; I was starting to search for the reasons as to why I wasn't happy. As I searched, I found my answers weren't concerned on how I could have given her and her child a better life, instead it was about realizing I was giving all of myself unconditionally and the love wasn't being reciprocated.

If I had not looked into myself and asked these questions, I may have never started learning how to stop blaming myself. When I cleared the fog of blame, I saw clearly that I wasn't any of the things that I was accused of being… Simply put, I just wasn't who she wanted to be with and that was the core of the truth I needed to face.

When you begin to look at blame and the many forms it arrives in, you begin to learn whether or not that blame is rooted in thoughts or reality.

My sage friend always repeated the phrase "Whatever you point at is something that you are avoiding or must work at." I understand this as whenever I choose to blame, I give away my power to what I am choosing to blame. My ability to be accountable for something within my own life escapes me and the opportunity is lost when I choose to make someone else accountable in lieu of accepting what is happening.

If you blame yourself, ask why? If you blame others, ask how? Ask yourself if blame is an issue for you? And what is triggering you to enter into the blame game? Look at where you are activating or being activated by to cause blame to exist, and then be with it for a moment. Look at the weight of its existence. Is it heavy? Is it light? Do you want to carry it or release it from your space?

Blame is a road that when travelled on keeps us from being responsible for how we show up. It robs us of being the best version of ourselves. It is when we look at who we are that we can change, or accept the reality and then move forward with knowing who we are in the process.

TIME TO CREATE

Take a moment to look at who you are today.

Look at what you do in your daily life. What are some of the thoughts you have inside your day? Who do you spend time with when you have time to spend? How do those people make you feel? What is work like? What emotions do you have on a normal day? Where or when do you have them?

Start to look at all the things that you're doing; the things that happen to you, and that you are a part of with a curious eye.

List as many traits about yourself and start the sentences with I am. Write down whatever is real for you and try not to think about it, just write down what escapes you.

1. I am
2. I am
3. I am
4. I am
5. I am

BONUS

Write a letter to the future you about who you are using the sentences above. This letter should not be perfect, it should be messy. It should not have structure, it should have freedom. This means it is not meant to be grammatically perfect or anything that keeps you from writing without editing. I repeat: DO NOT EDIT, JUST WRITE. Write without stopping. Where you choose to write is up to you. It can be in this book, an app, or a journal. Where is not as important as when, which is now, begin.

EMOTIONAL STRUCTURE

Setting up structure for what is to come

Most of us start without a clue as to how to best cope and we enter the path of divorce ill prepared, without knowing what the first step should be. Others hire professionals to guide them along the journey, much like an onboard GPS, letting their counsel direct them on how to sensibly proceed and alert them to what's coming up next.

When you are lost and not knowing what to do, the issues facing you become amplified; they're loud and overwhelming, and can often disempower us from being present in the moment. When this happens, it can cause confusion, anxiety, and other uninvited emotions to be present. This is where having structure makes divorce manageable.

With structure, you have the ability to navigate the road ahead without having to react to it. While every divorce is unique, there is a structure that exists to keep you aware of what works for you.

I remember crying uncontrollably when I knew divorce was to become my new reality. The crying stemmed from not knowing. I didn't know who to speak with, or where to go where I would feel safe. I was petrified of losing everything I had spent a lifetime building. Inside my mind, I imagined the worst and in the process felt paralyzed. The white picket fence dream had shattered and turned into a barbed wire nightmare I couldn't escape.

It wasn't until I created my structure and began to apply the tools before I could get a sense of direction. When tools become accessible a shift in your day to day occurs and this is when you begin to rinse and repeat what you have control over while you prepare for what you do not have control over.

Structure: Building Your Plan

Seeing the bigger picture begins with understanding the process. It is my belief that we can break down the divorce process into these three areas: Emotional, Physical, and Legal. These areas are what could constitute all the areas of life which need managing or mindfulness within the divorce process. I say this because each one of these needs to be dealt with, arranged, or created to make the divorce process manageable from an individual perspective. But before we dive into this, let me contribute a clearer definition of each area in the context they will be referred to in this book.

With **Emotional** Structure we will distinguish the emotions we will go through, and how we behave inside them. We will look at the stages of emotions available to us and how that could affect our divorce process. Exploring some of the pitfalls which could arise while providing examples and tools on how to manage them.

With **Physical Structure** we will distinguish the different ways of manifesting physical structures, such as, gyms, courses, classes, etc… We will also discuss the importance of why they should exist. We will explore what is available and the cost of not having this in existence, as well as, the benefits of having it exist.

With **Legal Structure**, we will look at the many legal options available to you and the various steps needed to take towards completing a divorce. Offering you a sense of what each option may look like before beginning to take legal actions.

The intention is to provide you a checklist. With the hope that when done properly will provide a timeline in which you can expect to have what you need completed. From legal advice to frame of mind and everything in between. When you have a sense of direction, your mind tends to wander less and achieve more. This is the goal.

Entering any situation where you arrive unprepared for, the panic and overwhelming emotions can take over and cause you to miss out on seeing a desired outcome. However, with conscious action you can build the structures to support you in shaping the future you want. Structures with stronger foundations enable good decision making.

It is when we are not organized, ready, or aware of what is happening or about to happen where we miss out on seeing what is possible. This is why building a mindful structure of Emotional, Physical, and Legal is a good start in our search for what needs to be completed to have the divorce be final while our sense of self explored, listened to, and acknowledged.

Emotional Structure

As you journey through your divorce, your emotions will naturally fluctuate, and your state of mind can shift radically as you endeavor to respond to the latest events and communications with your ex. To have a clearer understanding of the emotions that are likely to come up for you, let's create a visual of what your feelings, thoughts, etc can be like inside the divorce process.

Imagine emotions like anger, denial, bargaining, and acceptance all get placed onto a rollercoaster—the biggest, scariest, most aggressive rollercoaster the world has ever seen. Then you are placed in the very front of this ride: Alone. The emotions are in the same coaster as passengers, but they are seated behind you. You will not see them, but you will hear them. You will feel them, and you will know they are there, behind you because they are constantly shouting things into your ear.

The rollercoaster doesn't stop: It's always going, 24 hours a day, seven days a week. So you never have a moment to rest. It has loops, turns, drops, and it will reset itself to the top once the day ends.

The ride always starts when you wake up, continuing throughout the day, and then takes on a different shape again in your dreams. This is what most divorces have gone through. Some for days and weeks, others for months and years.

What most of us learned after the fact and proved to be helpful in our healing process was knowing you can create how you participate on the rollercoaster.

Do you react to what the emotions are experiencing, how they interpret the experience, or, do you experience your own rollercoaster? Do you create your own terms, creating your own experience? For example, you are told there is no hope to get back together again, you have no money, and you are not aware of the divorce process. Let's say you're devastated and as a result you begin to cry without control. What do you do then?

An option could be to allow your emotions to take the natural course and observe yourself in the process. Take note of what you are feeling, and why. Observe where you are strong and know what actions to take and where you are weak, and not confident of what to do?

The emotional stages do not arrive in order, nor do you move on from them in a particular order. Each stage is an individual; each has its own process.

Having an objective inside the rollercoaster provides you with the ability to notice and distinguish who you are, what you are going through. It allows you to keep a watchful eye over yourself while your feelings are front and center. They serve you as a guide.

Observing yourself when feelings are running the show can give you insight into why you are feeling what you are feeling. Be patient and allow them to flow through you, then take the time to look back and understand what emotions were present, and what triggered them.

When you know what you are feeling, you can begin to understand why you are feeling it.

Denial: What to expect

In this stage, many things can come up; the most prevalent, the inability to accept. Some of us try to rekindle or force ourselves into making it work with our partners when in this stage, while others will refuse to look at the big picture and end up quitting, walking (or running) away from the problem.

This stage is blurry for most, mainly because it offers no clarity and it usually lives inside the initial notice or presence of an emerging divorce. It often occurs as confusion, rendering us helpless and without direction. The very name alone holds no ownership over the situation and, if not managed properly, often leads to bad decisions.

For many, it's the first stage of the divorce process. It is when you do not accept or see the present situation that you can be sure you are in this stage.

Other signs of this stage can be pushing back on the reality of the moment while using any tool you can lay your hand on. You try to make it work by offering change, or you make promises to convince the other party that the future will be different. You might convince yourself that the answer is within you and if you give them more attention, more time, something positive will rise from it.

You speak louder and louder hoping to be heard, never recognizing it is only your voice requesting a solution—the other is wishing to move on. To be done. To have it be over with.

This emotional stage has many faces, but ultimately it is the expression of "I can fix this" which tends to be the loudest. It is when we are not listening to what is happening or being requested of us when we are most likely to not see our denial of the situation.

While I was in this stage there was no real sense of what was actually real or what was fabricated. My mind raced a hundred miles an hour in every direction. I was lost and because of that I was forcing outcomes. It wasn't until I realized that what I was seeing with my eyes and hearing from my loved ones was different where I became somewhat aware.

Denial is the stage where you point the finger at others and not yourself, while also potentially harboring toxic hope.

Shock: What to expect

In this stage, you experience yourself mostly in reaction-mode, which can manifest itself in many ways. You could be frozen, or in frenzied action. You can panic, or be very calm. You can be many things, but reaction is the driver in this vehicle.

Your mind begins to review all the memories the marriage represents. You look at every detail as you scrutinize for a solution to a problem that might not be clearly defined. This stage reminds me of the feeling I get when watching a film and seeing a character recall their entire lifetime within a split second, like a flashback.

This stage has the potential to last days, weeks, and years if you do not distinguish it. Shock has the tendency to paralyze the person who is absorbing the information till something snaps them out of it. For me that snap arrived in the moment I started sharing my thoughts.

My biggest win over this stage was making the choice to speak to someone who had been through a divorce and whom I trusted wholeheartedly. I explained without filter what was happening, what my ex had said to me, and the loss of connection between us in as much detail as I could remember.

The advice I received from that share was sage. It explained that nothing I would do would make this feeling go away, and also that more feelings were heading towards me, and they were going to arrive fast and furious.

To move forward, I was told I would have to accept what came and observe how it made me feel. The advice was to do nothing with what was happening till I had a grasp of what was happening—until I wasn't paralyzed by the shock of what was happening.

So, I did just that, I observed and looked at the situation from the perspective of an observer.

Looking back at my journal now, I can see how using my tools and continuing to learn gave me strength and ease to navigate. Shock was the emotion that kept me thinking the same thought over and over again without movement, keeping me paralyzed. Then, in a flash, I understood why I wasn't moving.

I had to admit to myself that I knew the moment was coming. I was going to have to surrender to what my ex wanted and was instigating, which was a future without me. It was then that the shock receded, and my ability to take actions began to grow.

Bargaining: What to expect

In this stage, you may experience a strong desire to will the marriage back; to look at all the things that could be done, how you can change, what you'd need to do, and what the options could be to make it work again.

Rarely do we, who have gone through it, admit to the truth of the situation during a marriage in declining health. We tend to ignore the signs that are in front of us and instead we over compensate, impose, or mis judge the communications around us; often not hearing what is really being said or requested by the other person.

When your partner is voicing sentiments you'd rather avoid, listen to them. If they are asking for a divorce and request space or conversation, don't try to push the reality away. Acknowledging the present moment allows information to be shared and gives you a direction in which you can start building a future. Listen intently and make sure you know the difference between repairing the past and building the future.

You can begin to understand where your partner is heading by listening to their words and watching the direction they are taking. Regardless of whether or not you actually go through with the divorce, if you are here in the separation space, it's time to prepare yourself for what lies ahead.

This is the stage where most do not see the reality of what is happening. We don't arrive at divorce because things are working, we arrive here because they are not. Whether it is one person who wants out or both, a marriage needs two people who want to be there.

Bargaining is where you offer yourself up to your husband or wife, ask what they want, while you look for ways that you can give or take. It is where the individuality begins to be felt by both, and it more often than not offers more "no's" than "yes's". It can be the first steps of knowing or creating the new parameters you and the other person are setting.

This is also the stage where we can become frustrated and lost due to not seeing what is happening right in front of us—what the current situation is truly presenting. Be mindful that thinking like this (not being present and seeing the big picture) does not produce positive results. I invite you to ask questions over sharing thoughts as it supports listening, which gives you the blueprint to what the other person wants.

By listening, you can then take a minute and create what you are willing to accept, or deny. It gives you a chance to cultivate what you wish to bargain for, and also with. If you are not aware of what the other person needs or wants, then you are only knowing what you want or need. It is to your benefit to understand what the other person is saying.

Anger: What to expect

In this stage, you will be highly reactive. You become the boiling water in the pot that is spilling over the stove until the heat is turned down.

I highly recommend that you develop your awareness of what your triggers are, noting what causes your anger to bubble up, and also what makes your ex turn into a towering rage. Having an indicator or a reference you can notice or call upon when you are in this stage assists you in the awareness of being caught up in it.

When you or the other person is angry, bad decisions can follow. This emotion is destructive and not grounded. Creating from this space is far from a sound idea when moving towards a dissolution of marriage—in anger the floor beneath your feet shakes.

For me, I witnessed my anger flare up each time I thought of doing something to punish or blame. When I was in that state of mind, I could see anger was present. When I thought these things, I immediately got into communication with someone I trusted and vented my thoughts with a conscious effort to not edit what I was thinking. I released the poison that was fueled by anger into a conversation with my ally who was well aware of my intention.

Anger is an emotion that escalates quickly when activated, usually by the heat of the moment. If not harnessed properly, or thought of frequently, it can cause harm.

Being clear on what angers you or others, what triggers you or your ex, and how to deal with anger are highly valuable tools when managed properly. By taking the time to gain this understanding, you craft a shield which can protect your energy and composure when anger arrives.

Depression: What to expect

In this stage, we tend to shut down all the physical and mental momentum we have, or had. We surrender and become less active, so results are slow to move forward and manifest.

This stage can give way to emotions similar to those felt when we encounter grief, like when someone you love has left this earth and all you have left is the memory. Such thoughts can be debilitating when you dwell on them, however they can also be fuel when channeled correctly.

Personally, I'm grateful for having learned how to lean on my memories to navigate me out of depression. I was advised by a trusted friend to embrace my divorce as an opportunity, and in doing so I opened photo books, took walks outside my neighborhood, and I began to make actions around my depression. I placed myself in the locations I shared with her and remembered the good times. All phone calls were taken while walking when I was home, and in doing so I walked past locations with memories I had shared. I chose to make those walks an opportunity to be grateful.

Depression was substituted with looking at pictures and remembering the good times. These were conscious choices initiated by me regardless of what I wanted to do. What I wanted to do was stay in bed, thinking "why is this happening to me?" or ponder on what I did wrong.

By recalling what my past looked like I appreciated what I had experienced, learned to accept that it was not my choice to cease continuing the relationship. I was able to say goodbye in lieu of lingering aimlessly.

In witnessing my sadness and holding space for it, I'd pour my observations into my journal at the end of each night, noting triggers that had come up for me and my subsequent contemplations. Each pitfall I located was assigned an opposite action to it. And when I felt a loss of power, I called someone to share and connect with, rather than dwelling in my depressive thoughts alone. .

It was the actions I defined for myself that got me moving through this stage, inching towards the healthy future I ultimately wanted.

Depression is overwhelming, especially when it's fresh. Be mindful of what makes you depressed and assign it an action. Remember, it is action that provides you with results.

Here are some of the actions I built around my awareness of feeling depressed:

When I wanted to sleep and not face the day; whenever I wanted to resign and not participate, I would say out loud "This is an opportunity to create my best self". I would say it even if I didn't feel it, repeating the affirmation out loud made it real. I would say it even if I didn't get out of bed or choose to answer the phone. My promise to myself was to say it.

Other actions I applied when I felt overwhelmed, lonely, or lost were reaching out to my tribe. I often shared my thoughts and feelings with a trusted person, purging without edit, and most times, by the end of the conversation, my feelings were less consuming and more manageable.

Speaking provides freedom from your thoughts. But if you don't speak them out loud you will never hear how they damage, or build. Listening to yourself speak, or having someone listening to you speak allows you to separate yourself from the thoughts and have power over who you want to be, how you want to act, and the reality you want to live within your divorce.

Speak up and often, it serves you to do so within safe environments.

Acceptance: What to expect

In this stage, you start to rebuild yourself with intention. You begin to shape the future that you want as you clean up the residue from the other emotional stages. You begin to feel relieved that the past is exactly where it is, in the past. You start to learn from the mistakes and use them as a foundation for what is being created. You create with what you have and file away the things that you've lost..

For me, I created my podcast, this book, and many other things as a result of accepting my divorce. After journeying through the shock, the denial, and the depression to the point where I acknowledged that my divorce was real and necessary, something inside me shifted and I was freed from my mental turmoil.

In the relief of acceptance, my perspective blew wide open, and I realized I could use all the energy of my divorce and all my learnings to create something positive. Acceptance allowed me to take steps towards the future while looking to the past as a library I could pull references from. It gave me a platform to stand on, to raise myself up from the lows I'd experienced, and allowed me to view the bigger picture of what was happening. From this healthier perspective, I could also finally see what I was missing.

Acceptance turned the very energy that had been debilitating me, into an outlet for growth that could be shared with others. I hadn't set out to contribute to divorce community conversations or the depository of divorce reference materials, but when acceptance arrived, I realized the future could hold such a reality. I saw the positive and made a choice to participate; To embrace the experience. So, let's just say, you can expect things to open up at this stage. You can expect to see fresh opportunities.

I, personally, found acceptance to be the last emotional stage of my divorce; it was my graduation from the change curve. And it was an empowering state of mind to experience. .

You will know you have reached this stage when you are responsible and accountable for your life without blame or suffering. You know what others (namely your ex) do is their choice, it's their life. You are responsible for your life, and your life only.

Even if you have kids, you must take care of yourself first so that others around you can flourish. If you are not healthy, you prevent anything healthy growing around you. Allowing others to do what they want (regardless of your opinion of what you would do in their shoes) is freedom.

In letting go of conflicts and judgements, you liberate yourself from your past. And in liberation, you find the opportunity and energy to rebuild.

If you are still disrupted by your ex, ask yourself what it would take to accept their decisions. What it would take to be accepting of what is happening, the choices they make, and anything else that is devastating to you. You and you alone are the only person that can decide to accept and be accepting—and you're the only one who has the power to bring about the changes you need to make, in order to, arrive at the state of acceptance.

PHYSICAL STRUCTURE

How Routine helps

Routine is what happens after you know what to do and what comes next. This is important because consistency inside our everyday life will provide us with momentum, focus, and hopefully clarity.

Having a routine that you can turn to daily or weekly provides you with a structure you can rely on and build upon. The less you have to think about what's happening, the more room you have to create what's going to happen.

Developing new routines in your life provides a level of comfort that you can depend on, helping you to maintain some sense of balance as you journey forward in your divorce.

For example, during the first phase of my divorce, I was stuck in a mental loop of the same repetitive thoughts while moving along through life, I asked myself over and over again "why me?" or "what happened?"—questions that never get answered and perpetuate a never ending loop with zero positive value.

The moment I began to fill in my days and weeks with a new routine, those questions began to lose the fuel they needed to remain in existence. Once I was mindful of my train of thoughts, I began channeling my energy into things I wanted to learn or focus on, which broke the habit of thinking the same thought. Subsequently, I had more time to develop myself in the way I was wanting to develop in lieu of perpetuating the same thoughts repetitively.

When I attended daily Jiu-Jitsu classes, I was so occupied with focusing on my physical self-defense, there was no space available for the "Why me?" question to appear. It was a good hour of not being my divorce. I was present to the moment during rigorous exercise.

When I answered phone calls I had a routine of walking away from my home or where I was, enabling walking meant I was always in motion while speaking or listening. My conversations had visuals like trees, and a bustling city in lieu of my white walls or closed blinds.

When it was time to go to the gym, I would listen to youtube videos concerning divorce and I would educate myself in lieu of thinking of my divorce. Merging learning with physical exercise, I conditioned my mind and body to evolve as one inside of a daily routine.

Routine is a tool you can count on to keep you off the couch, away from your head, and moving forward. Till you achieve acceptance of the situation you are in. Routine gives you the opportunity to fill your calendar with events and activities that promote a healthy healing process. Providing you a place where your mind, body, or soul can recharge and relax without feeling overwhelmed with the day to day.

Regardless of how you approach it, time is always going to move forward. It is how you manage your time that will make all the difference. Carving out new routines for yourself, adapting to them, and being consistent are all healthy steps evolving your best self. That makes a huge difference for your well being.

Routines break down the vastness of divorce and the newly single life, into smaller, more manageable and digestible chunks. Providing you with an opportunity to grow as a person while you are in the process of completing a divorce.

How a Calendar removes pressure

When developing a new routine, they need a home, a place to exist so you do not have to go searching for them. Calendars are a great way to remind yourself of these activities. Reminders within the calendar are also a great feature to keep you aware.

Your mind is likely going to be consumed with your divorce until you train it not to be, so to minimize the forgetfulness that occurs when you're feeling lost or lacking focus. I invite you to find a system like Calendar or reminders to assist you in keeping the future scheduled with notices while you reinvent yourself.

When I applied this to my divorce, each of my activities had three reminders programmed to go off at a specific time of day. I had several reminders for each task, three to be precise. I would give me a four hour, a two hour, and a thirty minute notice. I even went as far as color coding the events in my calendar: Green for physical appearances, Blue for work related times, and orange for tasks to manage like visualization, bills, or learning. A process I still utilize till today.

What that created for me was a countdown that would pop up on my phone reminding me of what I was going to do next. The consistent reminders kept me thinking about the future in a way that prepared me for it— and in the early stages of divorce any healthy patterns you can establish within a stable environment, is a win.

With today's technology, calendars have become even more accessible, and easier to share with others. When you create tasks in the moment with someone and commit to them via a shared appointment, it adds validity to what you are agreeing to and it holds you accountable.

Accountability is important; it builds and supports your integrity, creating a solid foundation with others when they know they can trust you to keep to your word. Utilizing a calendar and committing to your plans paves the way to dependability. It prompts you to honor your commitments without putting any unwanted strain on your memory.

Journaling: How it provides freedom

The act of writing your daily observations onto a device, a piece of paper, or an app provide you with an opportunity to log your experience of the day, week, or month. It gives you a platform to release what you think and keep it for a later viewing. It provides you an opportunity to empty what is in your mind, your heart, and your existence. Like a trash can at the end of the week waiting for pickup journaling has the same effect.

Where else can you go to purge what you are living daily in a way that is private and accessible to only you? Where else can you place your unfiltered thoughts to be viewed by you or of your choosing? Where else can you be the most vulnerable in your most vulnerable time about what is most important to you?

I committed myself to writing daily about my divorce, logging the details of the day, specifically about my divorce. What happened in that process was beautiful. I ended each day emptying out my thoughts onto a laptop and then going to sleep without the worries of what happened that day consuming me. I dumped all my concerns of the day into a container that was time stamped and readily available to me whenever I would need it.

I chose night time so I could recap the day while it was still fresh in my mind. So, it became part of my daily process. I did this not knowing that this process would later afford me the opportunity to write a book about it, and also to reflect on my journey through the divorce process.

What I learned through journaling is that each time you write something or speak out, regardless of the medium, you shed a layer of relevance. Like an onion, each entry or share peels another layer off. The weight of the experience begins to lose its grip on you. The more I shared what was happening to me, or what I had learned, the more I began to move away from what kept me imprisoned, my thoughts.

Journaling allowed me to voice my daily happenings and leave them somewhere. Emptying my mind into a container where I no longer had to be mindful of the weight of my thoughts was freeing to say the least.

When you think about something long enough without understanding or taking action, it begins to feel heavy. Find somewhere you can place these thoughts so that you don't need to be heavy.

Here's a fun fact which was created with my journaling. By providing me with a record to revisit my past experiences, and learnings, I was able to negotiate a better spousal support after I had already finalized the divorce, it was reading my journal that afforded me that luxury.

You might not need or want to return to what you wrote, and if so, it can exist somewhere in a container of your choosing till you delete it. There, ready for you, just in case you ever do want to come back to it.

This is a comfort that memory alone cannot provide you. Memories that are not recorded tend to lose the details of what actually happened. The tendency to exaggerate or diminish elements of the experience run high, memories become blurred, losing their freshness, and accuracy.

I am not sure how your divorce will go, but can you imagine a world where you journal your experience daily? Having a log of every upset, every triumph, with a timestamp and date to go along with it.

At the very least, you would have a chronicle of your life, what you did, what worked and what didn't work from your own perspective. Can you imagine all this information readily available to you and your legal team? Or, maybe you wish to write a book about your process. Can you imagine that? Can you imagine your divorce making you something, instead of taking?

My biggest takeaway with journaling was how beautiful the process is. I viewed divorce as an end, when actually it was my greatest beginning.

Support: The benefits of having it

We each seek support in different ways. We are all unique and, because of that, when divorce becomes a reality, we quickly learn who are the friends we can turn to and the family members who will be there for us when we need them.

But we seldom know where we are free to talk about the divorce, or what we are going through.

I say this because it is important to have someone, a group, or a community to turn towards when you are lost—you will need someone to purge with, to release the poison with, and to share the victories with.

The first six months of divorce is the period our emotions are the most unpredictable. This is because everything is fresh, especially if navigating uncharted territory.

You might not have an idea of what to expect, which is why it is important to find support; to know where you can turn for legal advice, or who to ask when you need to understand something new. Having support provides this.

For me, I knew that I wanted to talk about my issues, I wanted to face them. I had no intent to run or hide from what divorce meant. I knew that admitting my thoughts and taking responsibility was important to me, and that I did not want to experience the cliche divorce. Which was; they met, it was love at first sight, they ended it, and now they cannot stand each other. This was not what I wanted.

I was committed to making this a learning experience. I wanted a frame of mind which allowed me to step into the uncomfortable while still feeling confident that I was making the best decisions possible. Without a support structure it would've been nearly impossible to achieve this.

The thing I knew and trusted most was a saying a friend of mine (my goto support call) always shared, which was "worlds are created with words". My takeaway from that phrase was that the more you vocally define what you "want", the more likely it will be that you nurture, develop, and sustain the day to day with that "want" in mind. The context of that phrase is as powerful as implementing it and then seeing it created. This was just one of the many gifts I received from my support structure.

Friends: Setting expectations

I found that I had two kinds of friends when I was navigating divorce: friends that had been through a divorce themselves, and friends who had not. They both meant well and did their best to be there for me, but their own perspectives gave way to two completely different types of conversation. Learning to be mindful and who to go to during my turmoil, or who to purge with became quickly noticeable.

Speaking to someone who has no idea of the divorce process and asking for advice on what to do next is not exactly logical. Friends have the tendency to speak to you like they know you better than you know yourself, like they know what's best for you, which makes sense. But how can you advise someone about something you have not experienced? Don't do it. Know and understand what each of your friends brings to the table in terms of personal knowledge when it comes to giving advice.

Listening to others talk about what happened to them will allow you to see something for yourself. It will give you insight into divorce. It provides you with another story, like a history book provides you with a reference to the past, so does a divorce story. It gives you insight into what others have done.

Ask your divorced friends to share their story with you, what they did, what they would do differently, but DO NOT compare their story to yours. No matter how much you might think your journeys are the same, they are not. We all, no matter how similar, navigate through divorce differently.

Remember, you are not broken and you don't need to be fixed—rather, you are hurting, and you need to heal.... And while healing takes time, the quicker you determine what you want to do, the faster you will arrive where you want to be. Allow your friends to offer counsel, but keep your goals and purpose present in your mind when you offload to your loved ones.

You are responsible for your mindset. They are responsible for being there. Also, consider that your friends have lives of their own and being there is a conscious effort. It might be a good idea to have more than one friend you can turn to in times of need if this is the case. Be mindful of the weight you are placing on your friends and how much they are willing to assist you with. Sometimes asking them outright is the best way to create boundaries and keep either of you from resenting one another.

Family: Setting expectations

All families, good or bad, are still human. This can be where you are triumphantly supported, or it can be where gossip swallows you up. As you begin to air your dirty laundry with the ones you are bound to by blood, be mindful that they are also human and that gossip travels easily. Unfortunately, sometimes, the people closest to us can expose our vulnerabilities and bring us down in ways we never imagined.

So, when you are not sure what to say, say nothing.

You should be conscious of who you can trust and who you cannot. When separations occur, it's natural for people who knew you as a couple to take sides. The last thing you need is for the person who you thought you could trust to share the spoils of your heartbreak.

Personally, family is where I turned for my most sage advice. It was where I had the most protection and where the advice was specific and catered towards me. They had watched her behavior, engaged with her regularly, and held a different perspective of her and how she was.

It was the advice I received from my family members that had the most effect in helping me achieve my successful divorce. I learned how to navigate through dark obstacles because of the counsel they shared. It was this advice that made the biggest difference when I didn't know what to do and would've done anything to make the dark surroundings disappear.

Because of my family, I reached out, listened to what I could do, and acted upon advice with little to no strength in some moments. Knowing my family only had my best interests at heart gave me the strength to take their advice without overthinking. I was fortunate.

I will remind you to be aware of what you are sharing and with whom. Just because you are hurting and lost it doesn't mean you cannot be mindful of what you are saying.

Be mindful. If you say the wrong thing to the wrong person, it can be devastating to your divorce. What you say today, can and could come back to hurt you in the future. Keep the sensitive information for the ears of the ones who you know you can trust without doubt.

Co-Workers: Setting expectations

Again, let's reiterate the importance of recognizing your location, your audience, and your motives for sharing what you share with certain people.

Work is work, your personal life is your personal life, and the two don't have to mix. Be mindful of how you walk into work each day. How you occur to others is important and you should take great strides in managing this.

Create what you are willing to speak about ahead of time. Work has too many situations that can hurt you. Treat it as a place where you can disconnect and be super intentional about something other than your divorce. Being mindful of this can provide you a space where you are distracted from your personal life.

If possible, keep the sharing of your story to a minimum while you're working, and if you want to talk about your divorce with your co-workers, then carry the conversations over to after work hours. Keep this space exactly what it is, work. Also, when receiving counsel from well-intended colleagues, consider who has been divorced and who has not.

Hired Professional expectations

Having a professional guide you in any area of life is a bonus, but it also comes with a cost. Decide what it is that is missing for you and use your best judgment when making a choice to hire a professional. If you do not know about the steps towards a divorce, or you cannot research the basics to find out, then hire a professional.

If, however, you're comfortable researching which approach is best for you in the legal system, then I'd recommend you do so before reaching out to a professional. Listen to podcasts, read articles, go to hashtags and search engines to try and answer your questions before you start parting with your hard earned cash. There is an abundance of information out there for free that can help you to determine your best path forward when it comes to the divorce process.

Also note that professionals are professionals, speak to them with awareness of what they do and what their skill-set is, or else it may leave you susceptible to getting the most of their expertise from a billing perspective and not a purpose filled one.

Divorce is a billion dollar industry—not everyone is ethical and kind-hearted. Professionals make money off of billable hours. You are a client, not a relative, nor a friend. Go in prepared and savvy regarding what you expect to receive from them. In other words, do your homework.

If you are experiencing emotional instability, seek out a therapist or similar if you can financially afford to. Make sure to address the areas in which you are weakest, being clear as to where you're struggling in life and what's making you feel unstable. Note the areas in which you feel you are strong. Be detailed in those strengths. Make a plan and hire the professionals to guide you the rest of the way.

If you cannot afford a lawyer, seek out other options. You have legal aid, which is free. You have paralegals which can only file the paperwork but cannot advise, but do so for a fraction of the cost. Find what's missing by identifying what you know and don't know about the process.

Professionals do whatever it is they are skilled at for a living. Be resourceful when you hire them, negotiate if you need to. Make it work for you with whatever it is that you are bringing their services to. The more detailed you are, the more specific and effective the results will be.

LEGAL STRUCTURE

If you are legally married and legally registered you will have to choose one of the following paths when going through with divorce. In the following sections, I will provide what I know to exist and did exist for me when making my choice, which will serve you as a basis to have a basic understanding of what to expect of each option. I will give you a brief summary of what the legal structure is, but ultimately you will need to dig deeper if it resonates with you.

My suggestion is that before you choose the type of divorce you'll take, do the research and learn as much as you can about each path.

This is what I believe to be the most important decision inside the divorce process: Choosing the legal path.

Also be mindful of who you, and who your spouse is. In other words, know the other person. When entering into the legalities, be conscious of what you know of your spouse and the kind of person you know them to be. Throughout your marriage, you have learned each other's behavioral patterns, sensitivities, and trigger points, and keeping this knowledge at the forefront of your mind can equip you for handling the difficult conversations coming your way with rationality.

When dissolving a partnership, both parties are becoming individuals, and in doing so they might behave righteously at times, which could cause miscommunications and conflict. The moral of the story is to embody the outcome that you want to achieve.

Regardless of whether you choose it or not, if you want to be accepting, then you've got to embody acceptance.

This is important when we consider the legal approach you'll take because when you walk into your lawyer's office you can be in the driving seat, the passenger seat, or the back of the car. If you don't know who you are or where you're going, you're in the back seat. If you know where you're going but don't know how to get there, you're going to be in the passenger seat with your legal representation driving. However, if you know who you are and your final destination, then you're able to drive the vehicle we are naming divorce.

Please note that in the following briefs of Divorce options, they may seem similar, and they most probably are, but in the legal system they are worded as I have provided. I tried to cover all the options offered and how they refer to them.

Understanding your legal options

The law changes frequently and is different all around the world. The steps to achieve divorce range from country to state, including the length of time to become final and how it can be prolonged. Learn the laws appropriate to your geographical location and also from where you filed your marriage. Get in communication with a legal advisor within your community and confirm what laws govern your divorce before beginning the process. This will be an important step and the foundation of your strategy. Most Attorney's will meet with you prior to taking you on and in that time you can ask questions.

Entering into something that you have no idea about is dangerous. Before you start making any rash decisions in this world, make sure you know your options— that you know what you want, what you know, and most importantly what you don't know. Don't just take an action without understanding the legal repercussions of that choice.

Contested Divorce basics

This is when one or both spouses dispute the divorce. It could be confrontational, passive, or both. When one of the two people within the divorce is not in agreement with the other. You are more likely to enter a contested divorce.

An example of this could be when separating property or custody of children. One spouse might be emotionally connected to an item and the other spouse also wants it. Both spouses might want full custody, or to move out of state.

Who is right or wrong is no longer an option. Although, who wants it more or feels they deserve it could take you to a court decision to finalize who gets it. If it goes to court, utilize the law and lawyers to figure it out.

The cost of things is not just financial, it is also time, and heartache. Evaluate what you wish for before making a decision.

Uncontested Divorce or Joint Petition for Divorce basics

This is when both spouses agree on every decision required to end their marriage. From the toaster oven to the house and the belongings inside of it. From child custody to child support and alimony. They both agree to all the terms for the divorce. This is the quicker and easier divorce process. Also note that uncontested can be contested until a final stipulation is signed by the judge.

Stipulated Divorce basics

When a spouse will not sign an uncontested divorce, attorneys will file for a contested divorce and attempt to negotiate a settlement. By filing, the other spouse has a limited time to respond or a default divorce can be given. Usually, the other filing is accompanied with a settlement letter that defines the specifics of the terms.

Do-It-Yourself-Divorce basics

This is exactly what the header explains: You learn the laws, you find the proper paperwork, you file the papers, and you do it all yourself. Please be aware that if you are not 100% certain of what you are doing, it can come back to haunt you at a later time. This option is not necessarily the cheapest option. It is, however, the most likely to provide the least guidance. You will have to do the research and learn what is needed.

Legal Aid or Pro Bono Programs basics

Being mindful of this does not hurt. If you are financially limited, then seeking out law firms that do pro bono work is an option. Consider using an internet search engine to begin your research.

What I did notice and what alarmed me about this particular road was the amount of experience legal aids have. Because it is aid or pro bono, the services rendered are gifting you guidance, which could possibly leave you susceptible to being at the mercy of the systems generosity.

Be very mindful if you choose this route; do your homework.

ParaLegal/Legal Document Preparer basics

Check what the limitations of your geographic area are, as some areas do not allow or offer this type of assistance.

In California, where my divorce took place, I utilized a paralegal. My divorce was uncontested and because of that we went with someone who was accredited in the para legal process.

Be advised, a paralegal can guide you in paperwork, but they cannot give you legal advice. They can point you in the right direction to get answers but they will not provide them. They are there to file the needed correct paperwork for divorce. They give you a list of what they need, you provide it to them, they file it, and some time later you are divorced. They do not advise or give any kind of direction, rather they expect you to lead the way while they offer assistance with legal checklists.

Internet Divorce basics

This is the internet version of a paralegal. You tell them where you will file for your divorce and what kind of divorce you will be choosing, then they give you the paperwork to fill out and you can either file it, or pay to have them file it.

Divorce Mediation Basics

This is when you have a mediator in an informal setting of an office space, or like, with a trained person to assist you in communicating with your spouse specifically pertaining to the divorce. Dividing property, child custody, and support payments are amongst some of the conversations managed in a mediation. Once the involved parties reach an agreement, it is then recorded into a legally binding contract/agreement.

Meeting your ex via a mediator being present can be a good way to work out the pros and cons of divorcing before committing to it. A mediator has no power to enforce any decision, you and your ex must be willing to compromise within your mediation session in order for it to be a success.

Lawyer Driven Divorce Basics

If you are able to hire a lawyer, they will personally guide you as to how to best move forward, advising you on every aspect of your divorce. They assist you from start to finish and inform you of the law. This is the most costly option and often is a necessity if your divorce is contested.

Alternatives to Divorce Basics

If you believe that divorce is not the answer to your situation, there are other options you can look into. Below are some of the alternatives available to most:

Legal Separation Basics

This option allows the marriage to remain legally intact while the couple figures out what their future holds. For instance, if you have kids and need health insurance to stay active, this could be a viable option. When you have something that will dissolve if you get divorced and you cannot afford close it. Filing for legal seperation allows you to separate without divorcing.

Conscious Uncoupling Basics

Conscious uncoupling is a lawyer mediation service to achieve legal seperation without filing for divorce. You both know under this there is no future for your marriage to continue, but you want to part ways with the assistance of the law in terms of asset management, child custody arrangements, etc.

This term is not recognized by the legal system but it does provide a sense of momentum for people who seek a way to break-up. Conscious Uncoupling gives you time to be patient and move slower in the divorce process with legal understanding, while tending to the details of finalizing a divorce.

Annulment Basics

Annulment erases a marriage null and void, declaring it was never legally valid. The records remain on file, but in the eyes of the legal system, it never happened. In most cases, annulment won't be an option a married couple can consider, however as the law varies from country to state, make sure to ask a professional if this is something you can consider.

Possible basis for an annulment can be legal age requirements at time of marriage, mental capacity, and concealment, duress, or fraud. These are just some examples where annulment has been awarded.

Alimony and Spousal Support Basics

Alimony and Spousal Support are similar, but different. They each have types under them with specific tributes that make them distinct from the other. I have listed below a very basic overview of what each reference is and how it is used.

Alimony Basics

Alimony is a financial support ordered by a court to give to their ex-spouse during or after a separation or divorce.

Permanent Alimony Basics

This provision becomes effective once there is a dissolution of marriage or a judicial separation. It is only accepted in certain states within the United States and certainly the laws surrounding this will vary around the world. This is generally reserved for spouses who are not able to support themselves. Payments can be made in a lump sum or distributed throughout time.

Temporary Alimony Basics

This is ordered during a divorce that is pending. It allows the lower earning spouse to maintain themself until trial. This is a short term solution.

Lump-sum Basics

This is a spousal support payment paid in one lump sum of the entire amount of alimony that would be owed over a determined period of time. This has many pros and cons attached to it for obvious reasons, the con being that once it is paid it becomes difficult to retrieve if something happens. A popular pro to this is the certainty of not owing further.

Rehabilitative Basics

This is support given to a dependent spouse for a relatively short period of time to better themselves through education, or otherwise, so as to achieve financial independence. This approach is best when a spouse is expected to become self sufficient by a certain time.

Reimbursement Basics

This is reimbursement to a spouse who is entitled to recoup payment for any assistance they may have contributed to the other spouse.

Transitional Basics

This financial compensation is awarded when the ramifications of the divorce force one of you to adapt to new living conditions which incur expenses. An example of such support would be: child care, medical assistance, or moving costs incurred through residency relocation.

Compensatory Allowance Basics

This is money claimed by one party to compensate for financial loss or intangible hardship suffered within the marriage. A potential scenario that could warrant this could be that one spouse intentionally caused physical damage to their ex's property or publicly defamed them by slander.

Non-Compensatory Basics

This is support based upon the needs of one party. Example of this is when a decline in living standards from the marital standard is present and they are financially unable to meet basic needs like monthly bills, etc....

Spousal maintenance Basics

This is the payment of support of one spouse to another with the intention to prevent hardship. Divorce often creates a break in regular flow to how things go and this is to compensate for that. This is the same as Alimony.

TIME TO CREATE

List several goals you wish to have completed within the next seven days from this moment. The goals can be big or small, you decide. Same as before, don't make it perfect, just do it.

1. I am
2. I am
3. I am
4. I am
5. I am

BONUS

Write a letter to the future you about who you are right now and who you want to be in the future. Same instructions as before; begin writing and don't stop until the page is full. Don't pause while writing, just keep pushing through and write down everything that comes to mind using what you wrote above as a guide. Don't worry about what it looks like, or how it reads. Don't do it right, or proper. Make it messy and concentrate on writing without stopping. Ready…Begin!

If you are choosing to not invest your time in these exercise activities, I invite you to consider that this could be an indication of how you're showing up in your divorce …

If this resonates with you, ask yourself if this is who you want to be?

The exercises are not going to fix what is broken or give you the answers, but participating provides you with options. The exercise is to have you get yourself into action.

Actions create results!

TOOLS

Why are tools important?

In this chapter we are going to look at the different tools available to help you navigate the divorce process. The goal is to provide you with an example of each tool, what it can build, and how the tool can be applied. The goal is not to teach you something you already know but to distinguish what you have available.

Being aware of the tools that are out there, how to use them, and when to use them, can provide you more freedom in your day to day and less pressure. They can alleviate anxiety, as well as the discomfort of not knowing what to do. When used correctly they can even supply you with a sense of purpose and know-how.

How would it feel to be confident in your sense of self? Not easily overwhelmed. Ready to manage anything that comes your way with a greater sense of ease. Making decisions with confidence all while having your emotions in balance. Each of these are achievable with the right tools.

Divorce is a lengthy process when measured against time. Identifying which tools you have and which ones you will need is a question that becomes difficult to ask when you do not know what you need.

The goal is to see where you need shaping in your divorce so that it becomes a more manageable experience. This will enable you to build the future you want and give you the freedom and ease we all enjoy.

Make no mistake, it will be your consistency and efficient usage of tools that will empower you to gradually move up and through the mental, emotional, and physical spaces that embody the divorce process. The application is where the rewards from the effort are shown. I mention this so there is no confusion that it takes something besides knowing to make an outcome become a reality.

There is no shortcut when it comes to navigating your divorce. The road is bumpy and sometimes we don't see the finish line. However, there is a comfort to be found in knowing what you do have power over and how to manage it.

Every tool you have, or will attain, can only be used successfully with know-how. The greater the comprehension of what you are doing and why, the more you can see, the more you can do, and therefore the easier you can navigate or build. The more you study your situation;the more you intentionally craft the day to day to give you what you want from it; the more time and effort you give to growing and developing yourself inside this process, the more likely you will be to attain the goals and discover a sustainable state of well-being.

Education is your biggest tool

When we know what we want, we have a goal. When we have a goal, we have direction. With direction we can start planning, and with planning we can then gather the necessary tools to do the job. So, when you define the divorce you wish to have, a strategy can begin to take shape. This is why education is going to be your biggest tool.

Let's look at a carpenter for a moment. They use their tools to build something they've designed or were asked to create. The nail is used to keep something together, like the hammer is used to place the nail. A carpenter has a defined goal when hired for a job: They have an objective and a purpose. This goal is clear enough for the carpenter to provide their employer with an estimate of cost for time and materials, and a timeline.

When the employer has this estimate in hand, the next obvious choice is whether to proceed, which is an agreement. Once the agreement has been made, the carpenter plans the work and moves forward towards the goal till completing the project. Let's consider divorce to be similar to a carpenter. We have the project, which is divorce. Pending on the laws from where you were married, the laws will give you the timeline. Now what we need is the tools to complete the job. Here is where knowing the tools you need begin to be identified.

Let's acknowledge you reading this book as one of your tools. You have read this far because you are seeking something. This book is an educational resource about the first six months of a divorce. Where else do you have a question that needs an answer or clarification? Do you have kids, assets to be divided, or wish to move out of state? The more you are aware of needing an answer, the easier it will be to know where to find what you are missing.

Using tools like this book to build the divorce you want to have—in lieu of the divorce you will receive without your voice being heard provide information that can only be found by reading.

Knowledge is king—while ignorance leads to anything but bliss—and the tools we use provide us with the powerful resources we need to make calculated decisions. To create your healthiest version of the divorce, you've got to learn about the process and understand the steps ahead of you.. Educating yourself in what you do not know will make decision making manageable.

Physical Activity benefits

When I was learning about what to do and what not to do within my divorce, physical activity was a tool I used daily to keep me sane. It assisted me in burning off excess energy, while I tuned into my health and well being.

I invite you to explore what tools you have available in this realm. What kind of physical activity appeals to you? Maybe jogging or running in the park? How about weight training? Aerobics? Yoga or swimming?. If you have limits with your body, what can you do to burn off the energy that's racing through your core? Do your research, find what works for you. But have it be physical, and strenuous enough that you feel the release of energy pouring out of you.

Physical activity is a direct source to channel the energy you have each day. The angst from encounters with your ex, or emotional black holes that arise without invitation can be diluted if and when you have a physical outlet.

I practiced Brazilian Jiu-Jitsu as one of my activities and I went to the gym every other day. I committed it to my schedule and placed my exercises in my calendar with reminders to keep me on track so I can keep the promise I had made myself to improve my health. When I say I committed to this, I say commit, because it wasn't something I always wanted to do, rather it was something I'd said I would do and I held myself accountable to doing.

Find something, whether its' an exercise or an activity, that you know will be good for you, and then show up for it whether your mental chatter agrees to it or not.

Commit to yourself. Invest in yourself, and you'll reap the rewards. Physical activity will release that weight your body takes on from the pressure that is a divorce. My approach was to release it and learn something new in the process.

I wanted to learn self defense and I needed an outlet for my anger. For me, Jiu Jitsu was amazing. It was the remedy I needed for calming my rampant emotions and expelling my stress. Years later, I am still practising Jiu-Jitsu and I am more advanced in my self defense, more confident, and have sustained my physical health.

Find your physical activity and keep to it. Be mindful of your physical capabilities and if you have the slightest doubt, speak to a certified professional about your body's limitations.

Training Yourself

Training is what you make yourself available for. A consistent regimen that you will apply on a daily, weekly, monthly (or something in between) schedule. This is your commitment to the goals you want in your future.

When you can define what you want to gain or achieve, when you can see it clearly and have the ability to paint the picture, you can create the roadmap to get there. It is simply a question of what you need and how much time it will take to get you there.

Most people don't see divorce as an opportunity to train yourself. But, if you take the time to step away from your situation, and look to the future, something opens up inside this context. When you can see the future you want, you can learn what the steps are to get there. If you can ask questions then you can find answers…

Training is the mindset in which athletes and intellectuals utilize their time to build. Everyone has access to training, but it is those that apply it who achieve the best results. So, consider that the situation which had you pick up this book already tells you that you have the ability to train yourself in getting to where you want. You have the ability to train yourself towards achieving that future you want.

Sports provide an outlet

All sports provide you with a physical outlet. From bowling to football, when practiced consistently they provide you a road where you can disrupt the thought process that occurs when you are going through a divorce. From Rollerblading to Tennis, from Swimming to Ballet, each sport provides an opportunity to participate in and focus on something outside of the divorce—they provide a space for you to concentrate.

Having an hour, or half hour of the day where your mind doesn't think about the reality of your divorce offers an opportunity to reset. Sports give you this opportunity, especially if it is team oriented and involves other players.

Single participant sports like weight training keep you isolated. They still serve a function, but team sports or sports that require your mental focus enforce a break from the mental chatter that spirals around your divorce. However, if you find yourself drawn to the treadmill for example, then I invite you to bring something else into the mix.

Something I applied while weight training that worked for me was listening to podcasts. Specifically where relationship coaches gave insights into the divorce process. These were growth opportunities that could be cultivated within my workouts. So if you're heading towards the gym, why not seek out an interesting podcast to accompany you? This way, your brain will be given a break from thinking while your body works to improve your physical health, so will your mental health.

Being active is good for the mind, the body, and the spirit. This is why I strongly advise you to consider incorporating sports as part of your routine in one way or another while you experience your journey through your divorce.

Internet videos educate and distract

The internet is the single greatest invention for helping us navigate divorce. You literally have no excuse to not learn what to do, or how to do it. If you know what is missing in your life, what's upsetting you, or have encountered a circumstance that you don't know how to manage, all you need to do is type it into a search engine and within minutes you will have resources presented to you providing some, if not all, of the information you need.

The beauty of the videos is the time it takes. Especially if you have a playlist on a platform like youtube, or similar, where you can contain all the material. I personally used youtube for most of my research. I had no real idea of what my options were at the beginning in regards to the divorce process. So, after reaching out to friends and family that had gone through it, I used the internet to understand the details of what was to come. Their advice became the keywords I used to find my content.

The beauty of the internet is that it offers impactful information at such a rapid pace. When we search for help online, we can find professional advice everywhere. No information overload, just content delivered in bitesize chunks which are easy to digest and create stepping stones with research and insight.

Via Youtube videos, I learned my state's laws on divorce. I learned what Final Stipulation is and the length of time required to stay married before the judge will sign the final stipulation. I learned how to identify my spouse's personality type and the behavioral patterns that I could expect to see from her throughout our stressful time. I learned how to build a strategy around divorce, and how to manage it.

The best part of this was learning while my body was engaged in other activities. Whether I was waiting in line at the grocery store, on the treadmill at the gym, driving my car, or on my bike rides through the neighborhood, I was learning.

Educating yourself on divorce is not difficult, but it does take intention. It takes a desire for self-development and commitment to your own well-being. I found that videos were a fantastic way to rapidly and efficiently expand my knowledge—especially considering my attention span at the time. I was riding an emotional rollercoaster the first six months and these informative bursts were a great distraction and an invaluable tool towards my exit strategy.

Self Care Examples

When we talk about Self Care, we're talking about anything you do which is nurturing towards yourself. Whether this involves grooming yourself, getting a new haircut, getting a massage, or simply taking a long soak in the tub. Self care covers anything and everything you do within the realms of caring for your mind, body, or soul.

No matter what's going on in your head and your heart, it's critical that you take time out from your turmoil to look after yourself. Finding ways to recharge and reignite your inner battery is critical to being whole. The body builds tension during stressful times and through self care activities you can facilitate the release of that unwanted pressure, and unwind.

I attended weekly, or biweekly sessions with a massage therapist during my divorce. What I gained from each visit was a reset with my body. We tend to not realize how much of a physical effect stress has on us untill we relieve it. Then we have an "ahhh" moment, where the body releases and the tension is soothed. Of course, throughout the divorce, stress can be freshly renewed on a daily basis, and after a conflict with your ex, the benefits of last night's massage may be somewhat overpowered and diluted by the new mental struggle. So as you're facing your divorce every day, be mindful to invest in yourself on a daily basis. Keeping yourself in the best health you can. Recharge your batteries every night so that you're topped up ready to take on everything that's coming your way tomorrow. Schedule appointments in your diary for your self care activities, place them in a calendar and keep this practice going. Make it a routine.

These are also self-care activities in which you can invite a friend to join you. Go to a spa with someone, go for a coffee in your favorite café, or go to a concert… all of these activities offer self-care opportunities to let your hair down and actually enjoy yourself in the company of others.

If you find yourself without another person to share this with—the internet once again offers a way to meet others via local social media groups and meet-up sites.

Books: Learn what you don't know

Nothing beats learning when you have the ability to absorb it. I read several books on relationships, divorce, and the legalities almost immediately upon discovering that divorce was to become part of my future. I began by identifying the areas where I was weak and had little to no knowledge, like the legal process and how to heal. I quickly found several books to address my questions on both topics.

The moment I began reading, I was learning brand new information. I was forming new questions to ask, new angles to approach my divorce with, and I was learning it as quickly as I could get my eyes on it. This process fills you with confidence and data, occupying your time and attention, while moving you in a positive direction—a winning formula in my opinion..

Whether you go to a bookshop or shop online for divorce literature, you'll find books tailored to the learning you want to absorb; an abundance of knowledge amassed through countless hours of other people's study and experience that is just waiting for you to tap into it.

Podcasts: Learn while driving or exercising

There are so many more options today, especially post pandemic. Myself included, I started a podcast addressing what was missing out there for me: www.DivorceTheFirstSixMonths.com. In my podcast people share their stories of what happened, what they did, and what they would do differently knowing what they know now. It's a buffet of episodes with knowledge around real life situations from real people that you can search through a la carte. You can pick what it is you want to discover and what pertains to your unique situation by reading the title.

Whatever podcast you choose, be mindful of keeping it in existence. I found my best times to digest this information was while I was driving to and from places. I focused on the road and seeing all the many suggestions being shared. It was soothing and informative to hear how similar my story was to so many others. It was comforting to know that what I was going thru was not so unique. It felt good to hear how others navigated their divorces.

Social Media: Learn from others

The world of hashtags and communities inside the social media realm is endless. There is so much out there for people today in the form of social support, it's easy to become overwhelmed by the amount of resources and knowing where to start. But it is super important to know they exist. I say this because these groups of people have an important ingredient, they have people who are on the other side of the divorce. The side that creates.

I started using Instagram during my divorce and it provided me with endless information and entertainment on a daily basis. However, a word of caution, be careful to not get lost inside it; learn to be specific about what you wish to learn and when you find the people sharing that content, follow them. You can start with me if you like. You can find me on instagram @divorceTF6M or facebook @ divorcethefirstsix.

Meditation: A tool for visualization

If you're not already practicing meditation, this a tool that you can utilize to create balance. It provides a wide array of positive mental and physical reinforcements towards healing. Even 20 minutes per day can bring about results in mind, body, and soul areas of life unimaginable.

There are many ways in which you can meditate, many methods. Finding one which works for you begins with learning the various ways you can practice it. Once you find a method, my suggestion is that you apply it daily, even if it is just 5 minutes.

My method during the divorce often had me practice this at the start of my day: Once the day began and my eyes opened to greet the day, knowing that returning to sleep was not an option. I would then close my eyes once again, but this time ready to greet the day. I would breathe in through my nose, and then out through my mouth as I envisioned myself inside an empty movie theater, looking upon the large screen with nothing on it.

Soon, the screen was whatever my thoughts were at that moment: or relevant to that day. I would view what I was thinking, why I was thinking it, like I was sitting in the audience observing a hollywood film of my own life. This would go on for a couple of minutes: a stream of free flowing consciousness. Each day different, but everyday unpredictable.

When you sit still and allow your thoughts to be seen and listened to without any action other to observe, we get to see how the mind makes connections. We have an opportunity to look at the characters and situations the movie our life has. We get to experience where we feel strong and where we feel weak. We get a chance to observe, which is both beautiful and scary at the same time.

In the last moments of the exercise, I would envision what I wanted to achieve, and how I wanted to achieve it. Then, I would affirm to myself that I am worthy of being loved, that I am loved, and that I was safe and exactly where I needed to be. I would say this to myself out loud so that I could hear my voice. I would then smile, open my eyes and begin my day.

What I created inside this pattern was a platform for me to stand on each morning. Building this foundation, this repetitive pattern gave me the context for my daily life. I would do this regardless of how I felt. I would do it if I didn't believe it, or did. I generated these actions each morning, no matter whether I initially woke up feeling sad, angry, or any other emotion.

A huge benefit of these actions was that it enabled me to actively focus on creating a future, instead of reacting to the present. I was toasting my bread before making a delicious sandwich called life and packing it with all the fixin's that day was going to offer. Yet, that was not my biggest takeaway from doing those actions.

The biggest takeaway was in seeing that I followed through with the commitment I'd made to myself, even when I did not want to. It was knowing that I had started my day in the best way that I knew how, and I had honored my word to myself … That was the gold at the end of that rainbow.

Meditation will provide you with an endless stream of consciousness to look upon. It will never not have something for you to see, but it will be your choosing to knock on the door. It will be your choice to practice it.

DIVORCE THE FIRST SIX MONTHS WITH PETER MAESTREY

STRATEGY

The future starts today

This is a plan of action or policy designed to achieve a major or overall aim.

The divorce process has many steps to it. You have to file paperwork, figure out living conditions: who gets what, etc… Divorce is very unpredictable till you reach the final stipulation, and even then things can go in unanticipated directions.

I remember several moments where I just closed my laptop because the thought of how many things needed attention consumed me. All I could think of was: I am not smart enough to do this, I'm going to fail. I understood I had to get to a place where I could see the future, but I struggled to get there—the only thing I could see was how little I knew.

Naturally, this is where the road began. I wrote down what I did not know. listing all the steps I had no clue on what to do. I started to identify the knowledge which was missing, because when you know what is missing, the steps become about learning them, and in the process finding the help you need.

This road will have both disappointments and victories, and you'll have to regularly realign your expectations, ultimately focusing on what you need over what you want.

Getting started with a strategy

To get started with developing your strategy, the first action I recommend you take is defining a clear set of priorities for your divorce. What are the key things that you want to achieve for yourself through the process? Make a list. Once your list starts to take shape, go through and prioritize each point you've written and highlight whether it's a 'Must Have', 'Should Have', or 'Nice to Have' requirement.

For me, my highest priorities were that I wanted to dissolve our marriage in a way that was fair to both of us. I wanted to be supportive. I was committed to learning from my divorce and becoming a healthier version of myself; I wanted to understand where I was responsible so I could take the necessary steps to sort my sh** out.

My goals were pillars I could build upon and gave me access towards an aligned behavior. Whatever the situation was, or how my spouse would show up, I was always prepared because my goals were defined. I had a foundation to stand on and more importantly, to speak from.

This is what shaped my strategy and gave me strength and reason around each decision. It was knowing what I wanted that showed me the steps. It was the steps that gave me the action, and it was the actions that gave me the results. When you have a strategy, you define the path you'll walk on. From that point on it becomes a continuation of placing one foot in front of the other as each day passes.

Balance within our mind, body, and soul

When you take the time to practice self-care activities which cater for the three elements of your being, you take control of your overall health. This makes your physical, spiritual, and mental well-being a priority… And let's face it, if you don't make an effort to look after yourself; if you don't take the time to nurture yourself through this huge change in life, you simply prolong your recovery time. Learn to acknowledge yourself and where you are inside of having balance. Make time to see and feel. Make time to have this present for you, to exist. This is where you shine. Where you build from. It is important if not vital to having a strategy work.

Oversharing in conversation

Oversharing can expose us, leaving us vulnerable to others. Be mindful of what you are saying to people and how they are associated with your divorce.

It is not only the conversation that you have today that affects your outcome, it is the conversation you had a week ago, or a year ago that could be the deciding factor on whether you keep the home or have visitation rights with the kids.

The best advice I was ever given was to stay silent and do nothing when you are not sure of what to do. I stopped sharing my feelings and reflections with my ex after serving her with divorce papers, from that point on, our divorce was in motion and I needed to protect myself —my silence was my sheild.

Speaking out loud

All things spoken could be considered in a court of law. The greatest weapon your spouse will have against you is information. I present this as a battle because regardless of what you may believe or wish, it is. You are either battling your emotions, the choices being presented, or the reality of not being with someone you vowed to spend the rest of your life with.

So, be mindful of your surroundings, the volume in which you speak, and who you speak with. Don't vent to those that you are not totally comfortable with. If you have the slightest doubt over confidentiality, grab a tape recorder and speak into it, having a conversation with yourself in lieu of sharing with someone who could use those words against you in the future is safer. You can always choose afterwards if you wish to have that conversation.

Knowing who to trust is not always an easy task. However, with awareness of the potential dangers in oversharing, you can ensure that when you do talk with others, you do so mindfully, avoiding recklessly unleashing your emotions in the heat of a moment. Remember to protect yourself.

Speaking out loud was my most effective way of getting out the toxic thoughts I had. As I remember now all the conversations I had with people who later used my words against me, I recall how I needed to unload the heaviness of my mind at those times. I also see the effectiveness of speaking into my voice recorder and then playing back my recordings.

When I listened to my monologues I found I had new reflections, questions, and ideas arriving with me in response to my words. My perception widening with every recording I made, I found my conversations with myself were a hundred times more effective than talking with acquaintances who could possibly hurt me.

Identifying your strengths and weaknesses

Are you aware of what your strengths and weaknesses are? Do you understand them? Do you know what triggers them? Developing your self-awareness can assist you in identifying how to manage communication. I invite you to write down your strengths and weaknesses on a piece of paper. You can add to it, or subtract from it throughout your divorce. But for now, place them where you can see them. I believe it will be a great resource towards assisting you to remain cool, calm, and collective in every situation from getting divorced to being divorced.

I journaled daily and this helped me to learn how if I was being gas-lighted, without needing to question it or investigate further. I had written down what she had said and was able to see how she shifted it after. I also didn't share with her that I knew she was doing it, instead I used it in my strategy towards the divorce.

In my weaknesses (which was being in the moment with her, realtime), I was initially sharing my information with her in detail. However, I quickly came to understand that during these conversations, I was giving her power while ultimately draining my own. It took a lot for me to realize that the person I had previously trusted above all others, now had become the person I could trust the least.

Thankfully, because of journaling, my awareness expanded to the point where I saw the changes I needed to make and began to offer her less information. I conversed with her when necessary, but I did so cautiously and concisely, without divulging everything. In removing my heart from my sleeve when I was with her, I protected it.

It was not easy to identify my strengths and weaknesses. Having to look at yourself objectively you tend to build the best version of yourself without flaws. So, travel outside yourself, to your trusted circles to ask what they observe your strengths and weaknesses to be. listen to what they have to say and then use their feedback when building your strategy for divorce and self-development..

Goals provide momentum and direction

I want you to think of the word "goal" as the final product of your divorce. What is the ideal outcome for you? How do you want your life to be—not how you think it will be because of X, Y, and Z—but how would you like it to be? What will it take for you to be happy? What will it take for you to be more than okay? How will the goal be achieved?

Knowing what you want to gain from your divorce will give you the road to travel on. Having defined goals and keeping them in mind on a daily basis helps to keep our tools sharp as we get closer to our divorce's finish-line.

In my story, my main goal was to keep my home— a house we had purchased together. When the time came to declare what we each wanted, I first listened to her preferences and then built my strategy around her wants. In the end, the fair trade for me to keep the house was to surrender the business. Fun Fact: I didn't want the business. It wasn't in my goals. It was actually something I wanted to give up.

Because I had stopped sharing my information naively, I was able to position this into my divorce settlement without it being used against me.

The point to emphasize is the importance of having a goal. Without it, you are wandering aimlessly and not actively generating the outcome you wish to have. I believed I had two choices in my divorce: create what I wanted, or react to what was happening around me.

The choice is yours as to how you wish to go forward, but I want you to consider that when you have a goal, at the very least, you have an idea of what you want or need.

Mapping the Divorce

How do we plan our divorce, let alone map it out. Most people just wing it, they persevere and take it as it comes, reacting to daily life without planning for the future. Mapping out your divorce will allow you freedom. Knowing gives you freedom to create, to plan, to react, and to freestyle.

The main reason I call my podcast Divorce: The First Six Months is because in California, where my marriage and divorce took place, you are obligated to stay married for six months before the judge awards the final stipulation. Regardless of how you feel about it, you must wait six months before being declared single in the eyes of Californian law.

So, I mapped out what I felt those six months should look like. I utilized all the information I had in my possession, like my strengths and weaknesses, to identify the things that I needed in order to continue my journey and also to keep my mind sane.

I mapped out the legal steps, the financial disclosures, the assets, the living conditions, and all the other unresolved items on the to-do list. Using a calendar, I allotted time to every activity I needed to complete, scheduling my effort over the weeks and months to make sure everything would happen in a timely manner, without stress.

Overall, the legal paperwork when mapped out took place mostly within the first and last month of the process. The months in between were waiting for it to be finalized and making sure both parties did not alter the agreement.

The living conditions became an opportunity to expedite our separation and were adjusted to fit the terms of the divorce. My ex was given an incentive to move out quickly, which she accepted because it was suited to what she personally wanted.

Things began to fall into place for me because my goal was clear, my desired destination was clear, and the time in which to get there was clear. All that needed to be done was to follow the schedule of tasks already planned.

As a result, the pressure of what needed to be done was reduced. I was no longer triggered by my spouse's indecisions, or fear of missing out, nor was I affected by losing out. I was confident and standing on solid ground each time she raised a new request or changed in direction.

But this was only part of the process. This was the cerebral part of a divorce. Little did I know what was next would be just as important to understand, or to have a strategy, or create a goal around.

No longer having to share my home or my life with someone meant I now had to face something I didn't plan for or create a strategy around. I began to heal.

HEALING

Healing is not specific, I don't think there is a formula you can apply that will serve all of us the same. The time it takes to heal varies. How we heal is different. From the spaces we go through through to the outcomes we achieve. Healing breathes, much like we do, and it happens when it is ready.

My belief is that knowing the tools we have at our disposal, and envisioning the future we want, allow us to travel on the road towards healing a bit more comfortably, but when is always the variable.

The open wound that divorce creates runs deep, but it is up to you how your healing process begins and continues. Take the time to really consider what your life will look like when you are healed? Consider how you will measure it? How you will know if it's complete or need time? Seeing what you want in lieu of what you have can sometimes help you in moving through the spaces, but only time will tell when it comes to healing.

Once you have that vision in mind of what you want, then what you are about to read in this last chapter will serve you. It will provide tools to guide you, if you choose. Your healing is in your hands. I hope that in the process you utilize your greatest tool towards achieving it: Love.

Getting connected

When you are in your mind, the thoughts are loose, ambiguous, and have no real shape. They have no grounding in reality or consistency with time. They distort your perception of reality, making your interpretation of life, your perspective, a bit off from what is really happening. Sometimes you may not even know what for you is real and what is imagined. Thus, no real shape you can name.

Knowing this can become crippling when you are trying to heal. You may find that you have no compass to help you navigate or reason to help you become aware. If this happens to you, it could mean that you are not present to the moment. For whatever reason, if you find yourself inside this place where reality and thoughts are not aware of each other take a moment to re-create what matters.

If your in the moment and you notice this to be true, then look in the mirror. See yourself and observe the many details that your face has. Look out a window and find the elements of nature that when you look upon without detail, in detail, and be curious of them. Touch something that lives but doesn't have a voice and connect with something that is real. Get connected to something outside of you that is real. And when you do this, imagine the world and how vast it is, then look at the physical size that you are inside it. Imagine the point of view of an entire planet, and then compare that size to yours as a human being.

Getting connected to our presence has a powerful ability to put in perspective the wandering that happens when we lose sight of how much this world has to offer us. It is okay to heal, but not at the cost of losing ourselves.

Writing them a Letter

One of the greatest healing experiences I had came to me in the form of writing a letter. Soon after my ex had left our home and the waiting for the divorce to be final began. My mom came to visit. To hold my hand as a mom would when her son is hurting, and I was. We took a road trip to get me out of the city, I wanted to be around nature to reset myself.

We landed in a campsite in Big Sur that was every color of perfect. As we began to setup camp we quickly noticed the irony of life just across the creek and adjacent to us as two wedding parties were setting up for the upcoming celebrations. One being set up across the creek and the other in a motorhome adjacent to our tent. I remember looking at my mom and just raising my eyebrows in a life is funny that way kind of way look.

The trip began with a goal to go to escape the reminders of marriage and here we are in the middle of two wedding parties planning for two separate unions.

I recall that night to be monumental for me. I was running from the house that I lived in with her, and all the obligations I needed to complete. I did not feel comfortable anywhere and even less inside of me. I remember doing my best to keep it together while with my mom. Looking back, I did not do such a good job. Not until that night in Big Sur.

I was seated next to my mom, dinner was had, dishes were washed, and the tent was ready for the cold night ahead. We were seated in our recently purchased walmart chairs as we both stared into the campfire with blank expressions. Both not knowing what to talk about, both wanting the best for the other, but no words to really assist the other. A mom wanting her son to know that everything will be fine. A son hurting more than he wanted to let his mom witness.

It was then I decided to write my soon to be ex-wife a letter. At this time, it was a month after serving her. As I wrote the letter, my tears became the fuel for the truth. I could see in my mom's eyes the protective nature a mother has over her only son. So, she also began writing my ex a letter.

In my letter, I wrote out what I was feeling, how I had felt, and what she meant to me as a wife. I thanked her for the moments that she shared with me. When I finished writing, I read my words out loud, and we both cried. She then read hers, but her letter was not as nice as mine and we laughed.

We both tossed our letters into the fire, and with that toss came a release from the weight I was carrying. It allowed me to say what was inside me without the repercussions of saying them to her. It was freeing to see what was inside me, to hear it out loud. It was speaking it out loud which dissolved the relevance it had inside my head and heart. Prior to that moment I was hurt, I was in pain, and I wanted to stop hurting. That letter allowed me an exit. What I remember the most after the letter was the laughter that soon followed. Laughing at the memories, my naivety, and the many red flags now visible to us as we recalled the past.

As we packed up the next morning we said hello to our neighbors and started up a light conversation, which led to our invitation for the wedding that night, which would take place there adjacent to our campsite. The universe has a funny sense of humor. We did not attend. Although, It was rewarding to think that the night prior I had done the work to begin healing and the morning greeted us with an invitation to a wedding. It was a good omen and my mom and I acknowledged it over breakfast before hitting the road back to reality.

I share this story with you because no matter where you are in your process, until you understand what it is that you really want to say, you can exist as a prisoner of your thoughts. The letter provided me with a window to gaze out upon. Reading my writings gave me access to the power to get re-engaged with life again. To stop running and start building from within.

Prisons were not built for healing, so whether it is nature, big cities, or in a plane flying somewhere. Find where you can sit and write your letter. I guarantee you'll feel all the better once you do.

Ways to heal over time

When you research ways to heal you will find many recommendations and theories explaining the exponential processes. You will read guidelines about how to adopt routines and how staying away from toxic people and situations is vital to a blah blah blah. So what are the options we have when it comes to healing? Where is the meat and potatoes when it comes to healing? How can we break it down in the simplest form so that we can know how to manage healing?

The three sources that are identifiable, which we have a say over when it pertains to our healing process are the very three sources that embody who we are as people. The mind, body, and soul. These are the three areas where we can apply actions to regardless of whether we want to or not that make a difference for us.

The mind allows us the ability to distinguish, alter, and apply whatever we choose to make relevant. Whereas, the body carries out the physical actions, makes us aware of the damages, and informs us of our limitations. Then we have the soul, our most silent but powerful source. Supplying us with the overall link between physical and spiritual, our balance, our will. The mystery of known and unknown inside of each of us.

Let's look into what each of these offer us in the form of healing options.

Mind: Healing options

We are going to look at MIND as anything that keeps your focus. Let's recall some of the tools we have when it pertains to the mind. We can speak or write into existence what we are thinking, how we are feeling, and what we desire. We can place these thoughts onto something where we can read, review, and edit till we agree with them so wholeheartedly that we are inspired to make them our reality, our future.

We can do these things in a diary, a journal, a voice recorder, and a friend. We can purge the poison and the triumphs for others to become aware of as we continue to grow. We can absorb the same from others and belong to or create our very own communities where we raise our consciousness as we let go of what holds us back; as we pull towards us what makes us move forward. This is some of what is possible with the mind.

Body: Healing options

We are going to look at BODY as anything that causes you actions. From the back ache to the swedish massage. From the bath to the rigorous gym session. Let's recall some of the actions we can manifest with the body like the fuel in which we place into our bodies in the form of food. A decision we mostly take for granted or create excuses for, but seldom place a priority in times most needed. Times like healing, when we need it most. Food is the source of most of our healing from within and where we can make the biggest difference in our healing process. Another action is self caring where we allow our bodies to rest, recharge, and re-align as we push it from one day to the next. Knowing all to well that when we do these acts of kindness towards our self the healing process flourishes. Each act towards the body where you tend to it as a living, breathing life form is an act that tends to it's healing. Being mindful that your body is also alive and needs tending is part of the healing process.

Soul: Healing Options

We are going to look at Soul as the vehicle you travel in. Who you are being, who is around you being, and where you are being all play a large role in the design of how your soul is nurtured and cultivated during the healing process. This is why environment is so vital to your healing, and why the importance of understanding your vehicle, which is you, rests on how you care for it.

You can care for your soul in many ways. No one way defines the right or wrong of healing, but I would like for you to consider what works best for you. Be mindful of the space around you, the energy, the vibe. Learning to value and love yourself as the main goal.

Soul is where mind and body discover and explore itself. Where the residual of being kind or being mean lingers a lifetime if not nurtured and understood. This is where we do our most silent work, because language can never explain what love or hate really means. But with soul we can feel it, we know. It's unexplainable but we just do.

It is up to you to decide how you can best take care of yourself on a soul level, but if you're investing time in activities that will nurture what you know as happiness or peace, then you are going in the right direction.

Implementing a strategy for your healing

This is where we tie this all together. By listening to our mind, body and soul. By becoming aware that they need tending, as well as, attention and constant observation: we move with purpose towards our self. The work you do on yourself pays off and results begin to blossom from all the seeds you've planted getting to this point. You know how to think and bring actions to your self.

If you choose to participate in the proposed activities throughout the book, then you are going to have a sense of accomplishment, a sense of satisfaction that comes from knowing you are taking care of yourself. This will be your strategy.

As you continue to practice self-care, you strengthen and develop your emotional strength, your mental clarity, and your physical wellness while moving you into being the better version of yourself that was promised at the start of this book.

You are going to experience many challenges and unprecedented events during your divorce. This is why having a consistent commitment to nurturing your mind, body and soul provides a stable reconnection to who you want to be and the life you want to live.

The keyword to keep reminding yourself of is consistency. If you remain consistent in your approach to your divorce and the energy you invest in while remodelling your life, you will have the key in your hands which unlocks that healthy future.

Step one of this process begins with identifying what activities you will practice to nurture your Mind, Body, and Soul? Step two involves planning your activities and ensuring you schedule at least one self-care activity each day. Maybe you'll make an appointment with yourself to meditate in the morning before you get ready for work; maybe you'll go horseriding in the evening to get out in the fresh air, connect with nature, and exercise your body, or maybe you'll close your night with some journaling to unclutter your mind.

Maybe you implement taking a walk before breakfast, before yoga before dinner, or curl up and lose yourself within the pages of a good book before you go to bed.

How you organize your activities is up to you. You can change your journal, reschedule your practices, and alter what you wish, just so long as you regularly devote time to caring for yourself...

Be mindful that when you think you're too busy or too stressed to keep to your promises to yourself, these are the times when you need to ramp up your self-care activities instead of letting them dwindle down.

Step three is to honor your commitment to your healing and self-development. To see your plans become realities. Regardless of whether your motivation is low, the goal is what drives you forward, doing it regardless of not 'wanting' to do it.

I can almost guarantee that there will be times when you won't want to do any of this. But the fact that you have read this far, leads me to believe that you do want a better future for yourself. So, keep the promises that you've made to yourself and do it when you said you would do it. And remember, if you can't be bothered to take care of yourself, if you don't think you're worth the time or investment, why should anyone else?

Step four is to observe yourself and keep a record of what you are doing with all that is your life and how it makes you feel. Remember, these are all things that you are choosing to do in order to take care of yourself holistically—to take care of your being. By sticking to your plans, and working on yourself to improve your health, the rewards will be strikingly evident with time… And each day you move yourself forward, little by little, until you've worked your way out of turmoil and into a new and exciting stage of your life.

Imagine the life you want, then use that vision to design the path to your new future. I promise you that if you take on this commitment to yourself with sincerity, with time, your heart will heal and you'll begin to uncover the life you want and love.

Create or React: Generate the results you want

These two are so different from each other they are almost opposite. One has you driving, while the other seated as a passenger. But both travel in the same vehicle, to the same destination, with the same person.

Both start with a choice: Your choice. You have the ability to create or react to anything and everything, regardless of your physical and mental location in the world. The difference is how aware are you, of your options.

Creating the future you want is a direct reflection of the time and effort you invest into envisioning the future you want to achieve. Generating the vision and the goals pertaining to that future are what enable the manifestation of the time and effort invested.

Whereas, if you react to life, your future will be a reflection of what others want for you. You will be a passenger playing a secondary role in your own destiny. It's not to say that this reactionary style of living can't provide you an enjoyable future, but you can't actively develop the life you dream of if you're not creating it, can you?

By now you should know the difference between Creating and Reacting. Don't think about behaving one way more than the other, just observe your actions and then consider how you want to act in the future. Choose the course in life you want to take and move forward consciously towards achieving it. Be intentional.

Seeing the future and designing it requires intention. It takes awareness and focus. Like a child needs to be dressed, fed, and looked after, so does what you want.

You have a choice from this point forward inside of how you heal. If you have read this far it's nearly impossible to say that you are not aware of your options. You no longer have the luxury of saying you don't know how to either. You now have the tools to create the life you wish to have.

The results you wish to have are waiting for you. The choice you will inevitably have to make is whether you are going to create, or react?

IN CLOSING

As I write these words after spending so much time with you there is a strong sense of calm. A sense of accomplishment in knowing that what was went through could possibly make a difference for you.

My hopes when this was started have changed somewhat since the beginning, as I have. The process has been an opportunity to revisit the details of what was went through in the divorce, and in doing so, I had to really discover what was wanting to be said to you which would make a difference. A responsibility I had no idea or expectations of being so filled with love and self doubt.

In taking the role of author I had to accept that my say in the contribution to others, to you, had a value. Conceptually you know that all it takes is an action to make something happen, but after reading this book and now completing it. I sit here now writing my final words to you with watery eyes and a fulfilled heart because I know I have done what I set out to do.

The feeling of knowing this book exists and has the ability to prepare you in your first six months, besides you reading this far, is a blessing that will be cherished for the rest of my lifetime. So thank you

I wish you peace and love in your journey.

I wish you a beautiful divorce.
May it be filled with love and kindness.
For you and all those who share a part of it.

www.ingramcontent.com/pod-product-compliance
Lightning Source LLC
LaVergne TN
LVHW020936090426
835512LV00020B/3384